## This Book Has Been Donated to

St. Peter School Library — 1976

### by

The Benson Family
Russell Benson
Gr. 6

Students using this book should
say one Our Father and one Hail Mary
for this generous parishioner
who gave us this book.

# WHY YOU ARE YOU

*To all the wonderful girls and boys
who call me "Uncle Ammy"*

# WHY YOU ARE YOU

the fascinating story
of human heredity
and environment

BY AMRAM SCHEINFELD

ILLUSTRATED BY THE AUTHOR

*revised edition*

ASSOCIATION PRESS · NEW YORK

# WHY YOU ARE YOU

Copyright © 1970, 1958 by Amram Scheinfeld

─────────────── 4071

Association Press, 291 Broadway, New York, N.Y. 10007

All rights reserved. No part of this publication may be reprinted, reproduced, transmitted, stored in a retrieval system, or otherwise utilized, in any form or by any means, electronic or mechanical, including photocopying or recording, now existing or hereinafter invented, without the prior written permission of the publisher, Association Press, 291 Broadway, New York, New York 10007.

Illustr. #21, "Looks and Personality," Adapted from *The Human Heredity Handbook,* by Amram Scheinfeld, Copyright 1956.

Illustr. #23, "Tongue Tricks," Adapted from *Your Heredity and Environment,* by Amram Scheinfeld, Copyright 1965.

Illustr. #24: "Boy and Girl Chimpanzees," from *Women and Men,* by Amram Scheinfeld, Copyright 1944.

*Book design by Ragna Tischler Goddard*

Standard Book Number: 8096-1753-6
Library of Congress Catalog Card Number: 70-93432

Printed in the United States of America

# CONTENTS

1. **WHO ARE YOU?**   11
2. **THE EGG THAT BECAME YOU**   15
   *The "You" seeds*
3. **YOUR HEREDITY AND ENVIRONMENT**   21
4. **HOW YOU SPROUTED AND GREW**   29
5. **WHY YOU'RE A BOY OR WHY YOU'RE A GIRL**   35
   *How many boys? How many girls?*
   *Can't parents have boys or girls as they wish?*
6. **WHY YOU LOOK LIKE YOU**   41
   *The "look" genes*
   *Guessing about parents' genes*
7. **YOUR COLORING**   49
   *Your eye color*
   *Your hair color*
   *Your skin color*
8. **YOUR FACE AND FEATURES**   57
   *The "hairdresser" genes*
   *Other features*
   *How your face may change*
9. **YOUR BODY**   67
   *How tall will you be?*
   *Your body form*

**10. YOUR "MACHINERY" AND "CHEMICAL FACTORY"**    77
*You and the animals*
*Animal's advantages*
*How human beings are most special*
*Talking, reading, writing*
*Your chemical factories*

**11. THE UNUSUAL PEOPLE**    93

**12. TWINS**    107
*The "look-different" or fraternal twins*
*The "look-alike" or identical twins*
*Special questions about twins*

**13. THE WAY YOU THINK**    121
*Your memory*
*Intelligence*
*The retarded children*
*Prodigies*
*Musical and other talents*

**14. WHAT YOU LIKE AND DON'T LIKE**    137
*Your favorite foods*
*Clothes, amusements, hobbies*
*Your friends*

**15. YOUR PERSONALITY**    149
*Mistakes about personality*
*What you think of your looks*
*Certain personalities—and why*
*How personalities change*

**16. GETTING ALONG WITH OTHERS**     165
*Table manners*
*Being fair*
*What you wear*
*The way you talk*
*Getting along with others*
*The "bad ones"*

**17. BOYS AND GIRLS TOGETHER**     181
*Boys' and girls' games*
*Boys' and girls' clothes*
*Which are smarter—boys or girls?*
*Personalities of boys and girls*

**18. YOUR FAMILY**     199
*Brothers and sisters*
*Your other relatives*
*Your relatives' heredity and yours*
*Your ancestors*

**19. YOUR RACE AND NATIONALITY**     215
*The principal races*
*How races began*
*Your nationality*
*The true story of "John" and "Lee"*
*The qualities of races and nationalities*

**20. THE FUTURE**     237

**INDEX**     247

## ILLUSTRATIONS

| | |
|---|---|
| HOW A HUMAN LIFE BEGINS | 17 |
| CHROMOSOMES AND GENES | 22 |
| ENVIRONMENT | 27 |
| HOW YOU LOOKED BEFORE YOU WERE BORN | 31 |
| HOW A BABY'S SEX IS DETERMINED | 37 |
| HOW YOUR PARENTS PASSED THEIR CHROMOSOMES ON TO YOU | 44 |
| WHY CHILDREN IN A FAMILY CAN LOOK SO DIFFERENT | 46 |
| THE "HIDDEN" (RECESSIVE) GENES | 47 |
| HUMAN COLORING | 52 |
| HOW THE "LOOK" GENES WORK | 59 |
| THE BOY-GIRL "GROWING SEE-SAW" | 69 |
| YOU AND THE ANIMALS | 80 |
| YOUR "CHEMICAL FACTORIES" | 88 |
| UNUSUAL EFFECTS OF GENES | 94 |
| THE TWO KINDS OF TWINS | 109 |
| WHY TWINS MAY BE "OPPOSITES" | 113 |
| YOUR "MEMORY CABINET" | 122 |
| PRODIGIES | 132 |
| A MATTER OF TASTE | 139 |
| YOUR HOBBIES | 143 |

LOOKS AND PERSONALITY ............... 150
WHAT MAKES PEOPLE HAVE THESE
    PERSONALITIES? ........................ 156
TONGUE TRICKS ......................... 173
"BOY" AND "GIRL" CHIMPANZEES: THEY
    BEHAVE DIFFERENTLY, TOO ........... 184
WHO'S BETTER? .......................... 191
YOUR "FAMILY TREE" .................... 211
THE HUMAN SPECIES ..................... 219
MUTATION: HOW A GENE MAY CHANGE .. 220
THE TRUE STORY OF JOHN ............... 226

# 1
# WHO ARE YOU?

YOU are a very, *very special* person.

You may be too modest to think of yourself that way, but the fact is that there's nobody else in the world who is exactly like you. No matter where you may go, among all the billions of people now on earth, you will never find anyone else who looks exactly like you, or who talks, feels or thinks exactly as you do. Nor was there ever before an exact duplicate of yourself among the billions of people who lived since the world began. And among all the people yet to come, there never will be another "YOU."

That ought to make you a pretty exceptional person. And you are.

So you may want to know—and that is what this book is about—how did you come to be YOU? What caused you to be born a *boy*—or a *girl?* What made your eyes, hair and skin the colors they are, instead of some other colors? Why in some ways do you resemble one or both of your parents, or some brother and sister you may have —and why in other ways do you not look like them? These are some of the questions which may have been in your mind for a long time.

You may wonder, too, why in many ways you think like most of your friends do, but in some ways you think differently. Why do you say "Yummy!" if you are served some foods, but turn up your nose at other foods? Why do you like some people a lot, but do not care for others? Why are you especially fond of some TV or radio programs, or movies, books, games or sports? Why do you get thrilled by certain musicians or singers, while others leave you cold? All of these likes and dislikes are part of YOU, and it may be interesting to explain them.

You must also be curious about some of the unusual people you know, meet or read about. For instance, children who are born in pairs—the *twins*. And people such as midgets and "giants," or albinos (who have no color in their eyes, hair or skins), or persons with six fingers on each hand. And there also are those who were born blind or deaf or badly crippled, or with weak minds or sick minds (the insane). Then there are individuals with peculiar personalities, and some who are criminals. On the other hand, there are remarkable persons whom you may envy, such as *geniuses*, and others with brilliant minds and exceptional talents. You may wonder about all of these many kinds of people there are in the world. Perhaps you yourself are unusual in some ways— or some people think you are—and you may want to know why.

Yet in many ways you may not be so different from other people. In fact, most human beings are really much alike in the big things: their joys and sorrows, their worries and problems, their behavior with their families and good friends, the things they laugh at, the pleasures they find in learning and working, playing, loving and being loved. Whoever people are, and wherever they live, if you get to know them well you will find that your differences are not as great as you thought. It is important to keep this in mind. For to understand yourself, and why you are what you are, it is also necessary to understand other people, and why they are what they are.

Fortunately, then, a great deal is now known which will provide answers to your "Who-what-why am I" questions, and to what you may want to know about other human beings. The information has come from thousands of scientists in many fields. Some have been studying how babies are born and develop. Some study how children get their looks and bodies. Some study people's minds and behavior. Some study the diseases and abnormal conditions in people. And some study the differences among groups of human beings all over the world.

These scientists have found out the many interesting facts about you and other people which you will read in this book. In a way this will be a *true adventure story*. It tells about exciting things that have happened to you so far (which you may not have known) and some of the things that may happen to you from now on.

So let us start at the very beginning of your life, when you first began to be YOU.

# 2

# THE EGG THAT BECAME YOU

When someone says "egg," your first thought is probably of the egg you had for breakfast: a hen's egg. You also know (especially if you live on a farm), that if certain things had been allowed to happen to that egg, it would have grown into a baby chick, and become either a mother hen, or a rooster.

But more important in your life was the egg that became YOU. For every human being—and every other creature, whether elephant, mouse or insect—starts off like a chicken does, as an egg. But there is a big difference between human eggs (or the eggs of most animals) and chicken or bird eggs. In chickens and other creatures the eggs come out of the mother. Then she sits on them, keeping them warm, until they hatch and baby chicks come out. But in human beings the egg does not "hatch" outside the mother. It stays inside of her, and grows there until it has become a baby big enough to be born.

Another important difference between a human egg and a chicken egg is in *size*. Looking at yourself today, it would be hard to believe how small you were when your life first began inside your mother. Would you guess the "You" egg was as big as a baseball? A golf ball? A marble? It was much, much smaller—so small that if it could have been taken out and put on a table, it could hardly be seen.

Take a pin or a needle and make the tiniest hole you can in a piece of paper. Then hold the paper to the light and look through the hole. That's about the way the egg from which you developed looked when it first began to grow. What is more, the eggs that become elephants or giraffes or hippopotamuses are almost as tiny as human eggs.

Why is a hen's egg so much bigger than a human egg? It is because the baby chicken has to grow *outside* the mother hen. So the hen's egg must be big enough to carry all the food that the chick will need as it gets bigger and bigger inside the shell—until it hatches. But since you, like any other human being, were to grow *inside* your mother, the "You" egg needed only a tiny bit of food to get you started on your way. Thereafter, everything

## HOW A HUMAN LIFE BEGINS

1. *Human Sperms,* greatly magnified. (A sperm is about 1/400th of an inch long.)

2. *A Human Egg.* (Actual size about that of a period on this page.)

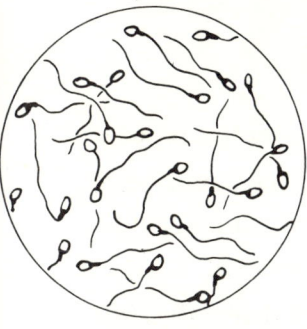

Nucleus of egg, containing "seed" package embedded in food material

Sperm entering egg

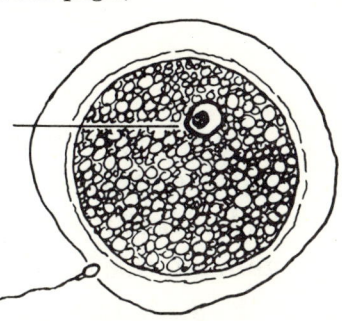

3. Sperms from father race toward egg waiting in tube in mother. Only one sperm can enter.

4. The winning sperm opens up and releases its "seed package." The seed package in egg also opens up.

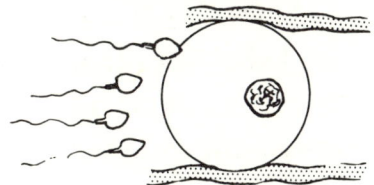

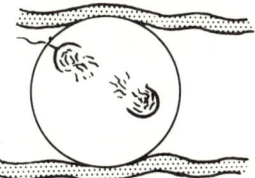

5. The two seed packages begin to work together to start a baby on its way, while the egg moves down the tube

6. The fertilized egg now enters the mother's womb and becomes implanted there

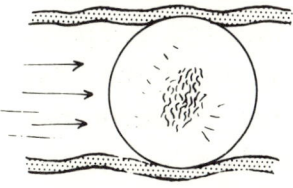

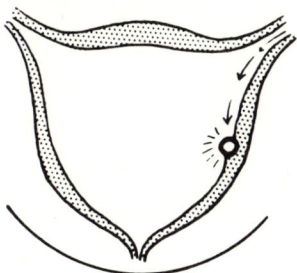

you needed until you were ready to be born could come into you from your mother.

## The "You" Seeds

The most amazing thing of all was what was inside the little bit of a "You" egg. If we could have looked into it with a microscope from the very beginning, this is what we would have seen:

First, before the egg started to grow in your mother, there was in its center a tiny, tiny "seed" package. (For human beings and other animals, like plants, also grow out of seeds.) But your mother's seed package had only half of what was needed to make you sprout into a baby. The other half had to come from your father, who put his seed material into your mother when they wanted to have a baby.

Your father's seed material was carried in a remarkable little wiggly thing, many times smaller than a human egg, called a *sperm*. Seen through a microscope, it looks like a tiny tadpole, with a round head and a very long, thin tail. A sperm swims, too, very much like a tadpole, in the fluid in which it comes from the father. However, not just one sperm was in this fluid which had flowed from your father into your mother when they came close together to make love. There were millions of sperms that swam in at the same time. These sperms all raced toward the egg waiting inside your mother. But the egg was so constructed that it would receive only one. The moment the winning sperm touched and entered the egg, the covering of the egg tightened up and shut out all the others.

What happened next was that the seed-carrying package from your father which the sperm had brought in, joined with the seed package from your mother which was waiting in the egg. The two little packages opened up and their seed material began to work together to produce the baby who was to become you.

Just what this human seed material was and how it worked will be told in our next chapter.

# 3

# YOUR HEREDITY AND ENVIRONMENT

"What do elephants have that no other animals have?"

This is an old fooler. Most persons might hurry to say, "Why, of course—*trunks*." But that's not the answer. (Some other animals, such as tapirs, have extended, workable noses that can be called "trunks"; and, of course, a trunk is also the main part of any animal's—or any person's—body, without the head and limbs. So you, too, have a trunk.)

What elephants have that no other animals have are—*baby elephants*. Likewise, each kind of animal has its own kind of babies, or offspring. And only human beings have human babies.

The word which is used to explain why particular kinds of living creatures (and flowers and plants as well) have particular kinds of offspring is *heredity*. The reason you are a human being is that you started off with *human heredity*. That

## YOUR CHROMOSOMES AND GENES

You, like every other human being, inherited 46 chromosomes—23 from your mother, 23 from your father. The different chromosomes from your mother matched those from your father.

Chromosomes from your mother

Chromosomes from your father
(See Chapter 6)

When human chromosomes are photographed under the microscope they are usually in the *doubled* stage (about to divide, to form two) and look like this:

A single chromosome (or part of one) when stretched out would look like this:

The *genes* are contained in the sections

Each gene in each chromosome has its special job to do

ENGINEER
ARCHITECT
CARPENTER
MASON
PLUMBER
DECORATOR
CHEMIST

In the paired chromosomes from the father and mother the genes at each place have the same assigned jobs

also meant you would have a human brain, a human body, a human nose, eyes, ears, mouth and skin, and everything else that distinguishes you from a cat, a cow, a camel, a chimpanzee or any other creature.

How does heredity work to produce all the big differences between human beings and the lower animals?—and also the smaller differences between one human being and another? For the explanation, we'll look again into the seed packages we talked about in the previous chapter.

If we could keep watching through the microscope, we would have seen coming out of the seed packages (the one which was in your mother's egg and the one brought in by your father's sperm), a great many of what looked like the tiniest imaginable little pieces of rubbery plastic, in different lengths. These are called by scientists the *chromosomes* (KRO-mo-somes, with each "o" as in "Oh"). Actually, the chromosomes could not be seen until they were first stained with some coloring matter. That is the reason for the name given to them, which comes from two Greek words, *kromo*, meaning color, and *somes*, meaning bodies.

If we counted them, we would find that there were exactly 46 chromosomes: A set of 23 which had been in your mother's egg, and another, matching set of 23, which had come from your father. Watching them further, the chromosomes could be seen to stretch out into strings, each with many beadlike sections. These sections are called *genes* (rhyming with "beans"). There were thousands of genes strung along on the chromosomes. And it was these genes which did everything connected with your heredity.

All animals—and all flowers and other growing things as well—also have their chromosomes and genes. Why do they turn out to be so different from human beings, and from one another? Because their chromosomes and genes are different. In other words, every kind of living creature and growing thing has its own special kind of heredity, and its particular chromosomes and genes which work to produce its inherited traits.

Each of your own genes had a special job to do in making you YOU. In fact, every gene was in some ways like a worker helping to construct, equip and operate a big new factory. There were "architect" genes which made the plans for your body. There were "builder" genes which began to construct your framework, with the skeleton, bones, muscles and skin. There were "engineer" and "mechanic" genes, working on your inside "machinery"—your heart, lungs, liver, stomach, and other inside organs. There were "electrician" genes for your brain and nervous system. There were "plumber" genes for your blood vessels, and for your drainage system which would carry out waste materials. There were "chemist" genes to produce all the different chemicals needed in your body.

There also were "sculptor" genes, to work out the shapes of your nose, mouth, ears, teeth and other features. There were "painter" and "decorator" genes to mix and fix the colors of your eyes, hair and skin. And there were "barber" and "hairdresser" genes to decide the kind of hair you would have.

Try to make a list of all of the details of your body, and all the many things your "machinery" enables you to do: breathe, move, run and jump, eat, digest food, sleep, see, hear, smell, taste, talk, sing, feel and *think*. Your genes had a hand in making all the equipment needed for doing these things. And your genes are still at work, helping to direct the way every part of your body is growing and developing.

But this is only the beginning of your "You" story. Other people, too, have "architect" genes, "engineer," "electrician," "plumber," "sculptor," "painter" and all the other kinds of genes that you have. However, just as among human workers—an architect, an engineer, a painter—one may do his job differently from another, so among genes of each kind there also are differences in what one gene does as compared with another. An "eye-color" gene of one person may make his eyes blue, whereas in another person the "eye-color" gene may produce dark-brown eyes. Thus, differences in people's genes can create any number of differences in their looks, bodies and minds.

(How does a gene work? For the science-minded reader, a gene can be thought of as something like a section of twisted cables, with many rows of buttons along its length. The "buttons" send out code messages to the cell in which the gene is housed, telling what chemicals are to be made or used, and what is to be done with them. The particular arrangement of the "buttons" in each gene decides what its code instructions will be. The living substance of which each gene is composed—the "cable" section with its "buttons" —is called DNA, short for *De*-oxy-ribo-*N*ucleic Acid.)

It is a great mistake, though, to think that only the genes which people inherit produce the differences among them. For in addition to heredity, there is something else which played a big part in making you and other people what they are. That extra something is called *environment*.

Environment includes everything on the outside which has affected and continues to affect the lives of people, or of any other living creature or growing thing. Your own environment has included what you've had to eat, how you've been cared for, where and with whom you lived, and all that you have seen, heard and learned, as well as everything that has happened to you.

## ENVIRONMENT

*For a plant*

It is everything
it gets from
the soil, sun
air and rain

*For yourself*

It is all the food,
care, training and education
you have received and
are receiving

So it is in a way foolish to argue "Which is more important, heredity or environment?" Both are absolutely necessary to produce living things of any kind and to keep them alive. If it were not for your *human heredity*, you could have been a cat, a kangaroo, a chimpanzee or whatever; and if it were not for your particular kind of inherited genes, and the differences among other people's genes, you and everyone else might look and be almost exactly the same.

But without a *human environment*—made possible by being born and reared among human beings—you would not have learned to behave and think as other human beings do. And without the particular kind of human environment which was provided in your home, your neighborhood, your school and the place and country where you live, you would be a different person from what you now are.

It is equally true for other boys and girls you know, and for the rest of the people in the world, that their environments as well as their heredity made them what they are, and will continue to work together to make them what they will be. As we go on with this book, you will see more clearly what it is in yourself and other people that is due to heredity, and what is due to environment.

# 4

# HOW YOU SPROUTED AND GREW

If you plant a seed in the ground, and start it on its way to becoming a flower or a vegetable, it probably does not occur to you that much the same thing happened when you yourself were started on your way to becoming a human being.

In the preceding chapter we told about the "You" egg with its little seed packages—the one brought in by the sperm from your father, and the other one already there in the egg produced by your mother. The process by which these two seed packages joined and began to work together is called *conception*. And it was in that moment that you were said to have been *conceived*.

That was only the beginning. As the next step, the egg was planted: not like a flower seed in the ground, but inside your mother. The planting took place in the thick lining of the special organ called the *womb*. You probably know that this is the organ within the mother where babies grow from the time they are conceived until they are born.

At the very beginning the egg was no bigger than the period at the end of this sentence. Then it turned into something like a tiny, clear-white raspberry. Each section of the raspberry was what is called a *cell;* and inside every cell were exact copies which had been formed of every one of your chromosomes and their genes. These gene workers were now busily engaged in developing your body. The cells produced more and more cells, but now different cells were turning into different parts of the body.

At first the material inside the tiny egg itself can provide what is needed for the beginnings of the baby. Very soon, however, as the baby develops, it begins to draw its food and needed substances from the mother. The connection between her and the baby is made through a long, twisted tube called the *umbilical* (um-BILL-i-kal) *cord*. When this cord is cut right after a baby is born, it leaves what you call the "belly button," but which doctors call the *umbilicus* (um-*BILL*-like-us), or the *navel*.

In our drawings we show how you looked at different stages as you grew. Soon one could see

# HOW YOU LOOKED BEFORE YOU WERE BORN

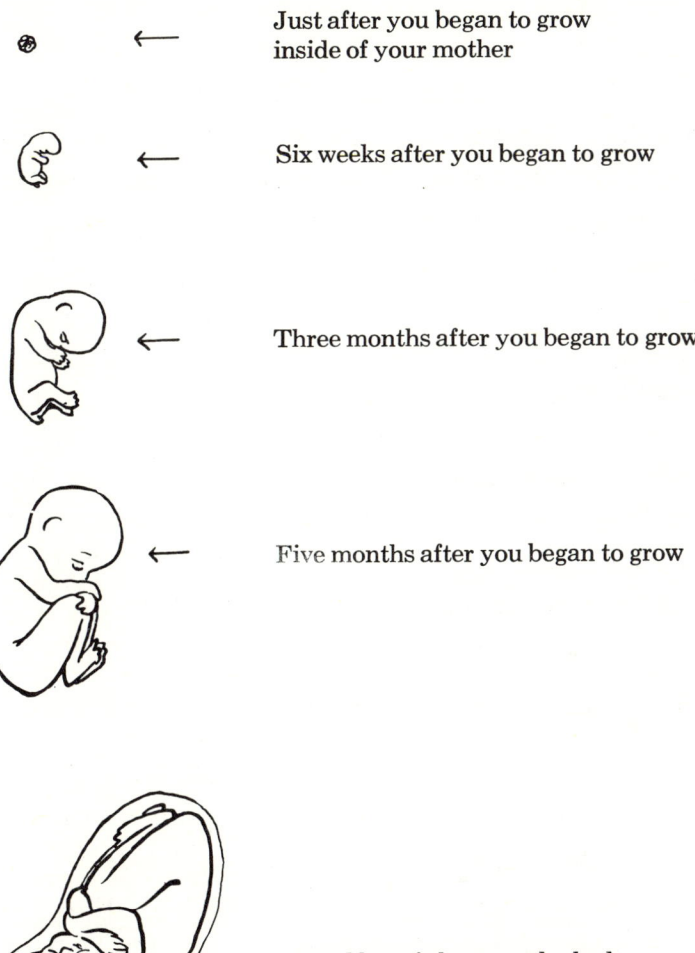

Just after you began to grow inside of your mother

Six weeks after you began to grow

Three months after you began to grow

Five months after you began to grow

And here is how you looked just when you were ready to be born. (You were probably lying upside down to make your birth easier.)

the head, then little arms and legs beginning to appear. As you kept growing, your eyes, nose, mouth and ears began to show themselves. Soon, too, there were fingers on the hands and toes on the feet. After about three months from the time the "You" egg started to grow, you really began to look like a baby, although still so small you weren't much bigger than one of your thumbs is right now. But from then on you grew more and more, and your mother could feel you moving inside of her.

Actually, you couldn't move much. Your movements were more like floating, swimming and kicking in a small bathtub. For you were inside of a sack filled with fluid, much like water. How could you breathe? You didn't have to. The oxygen—the part of the air which you needed— came in through the tube (the umbilical cord) from your mother. And you didn't have to eat with your mouth then, either, because all the food you needed also came in to you from your mother.

Usually, a baby keeps growing inside of the mother for about nine months from the time the egg is planted. Some babies stay in their mother a little longer, and some (who for one or another reason can't wait) come out a month or two earlier. When a baby is born much before the expected time, and weighs no more than 5½ pounds —much less than the average baby at birth—it is called *premature*. About one in twelve or thirteen babies is born prematurely. Your mother has probably told you—or will tell you if you ask—how long it took for you to be born.

At last the time came when your mother and the doctor knew you were about ready to come out into the world. And sure enough, pretty soon you did come out—with a big squawk, to let everyone know you had arrived.

If you have seen any brand-new babies, you will know what you looked like when you were born: all red and wrinkled. Your parents may have taken pictures of you then, and probably other pictures at different times later, so you can see how you changed, step by step. And now look at you! Isn't it hard to believe that you were once no bigger than a period on this page?

# 5
# WHY YOU'RE A BOY
# OR
# WHY YOU'RE A GIRL

When you were about to be born, your parents were probably wondering, would you be a boy or a girl? (You may have surprised them—especially if they'd been so sure they'd already picked the name for you, and it was a wrong one.)

But all the time everyone was trying to guess what the new baby was going to be, it had been decided at the very instant the egg had begun to grow in your mother. What made the decision?

In Chapter 2 we told how, just before the egg started to grow, there was a race among the sperms from your father. It was in that race that it was also decided whether you were to be a boy (male) or girl (female).

Here's how it happened: Among the different kinds of human chromosomes there are two special *"sex" chromosomes*. One of these is called by scientists the X chromosome. The other one is called the Y. A female carries in each cell of her body *two* Xs. A male carries in each cell of his body just *one* X, plus a Y.

Now since a mother has only X chromosomes, every egg she produces will have an X. But since a father has both Xs and Ys among his chromosomes, he can give a child either an X or a Y. In other words, a father produces *two kinds of sperms*, half with Xs, half with Ys, along with his other chromosomes.

So when the sperms race toward the egg, if a sperm with an X gets there first, it will join with the X already there, and will make an XX combination—a girl. If a sperm with a Y wins the race, there will be an XY combination—a boy.

Sounds simple, doesn't it? However, scientists still don't know exactly how the Y chromosome works to make a boy develop, or how, if no Y chromosome enters the egg, but instead an X is brought in, a girl baby will develop. What is known only is that the Y causes the baby to develop with all the parts and workings of the body that go with becoming a boy and a man. And if there is no Y, but two Xs, the baby is caused to develop with all that goes with becoming a girl and a woman.

The differences at first may not seem very great.

# HOW A BABY'S SEX IS DETERMINED

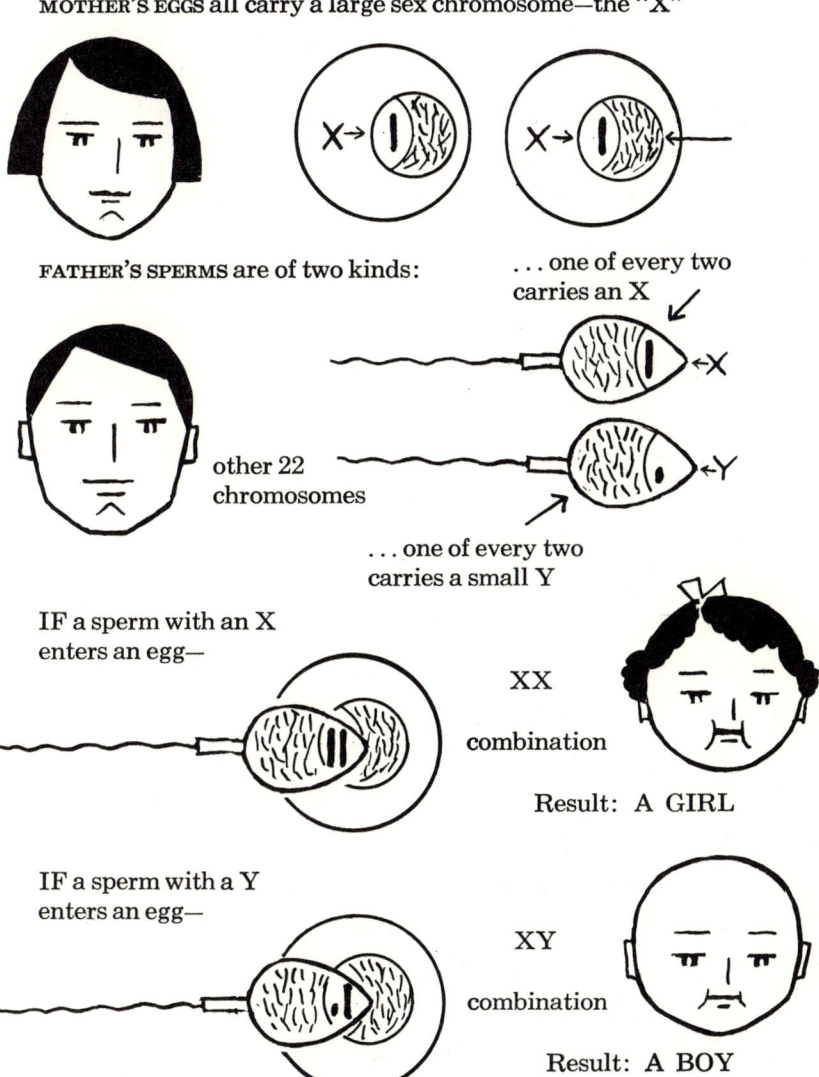

When a baby is born one can tell from the outside if it is a boy or a girl by looking at the sex organ. A boy has a *penis* and a girl has a *vagina*. There are no differences to be seen in the rest of the body, or in the face. But there are important other differences, just the same.

As we will learn later, the Y chromosome and its "maleness" genes, or the X chromosomes with their "femaleness" genes, keep right on working after babies are born, to make boys and girls different in many ways as they grow older.

## *How Many Boys? How Many Girls?*

Among all the babies that are born each year, there usually are about 106 boy babies for every 100 girl babies.

Why are more boys born? Your first guess might be that boys are stronger and healthier, and get born more easily. This, then, may surprise you: It's the other way around. Boy babies are often not as healthy as girl babies, and may have a harder time coming into the world. Among babies that die before they are born, or while they are being born or just after that, there are many more boys than girls.

The reason more boy babies are born is that the

"boy-making" Y sperms in some way manage to get to eggs a little more often than do the "girl-making" X sperms. So more boy babies are conceived and start growing in their mothers; and even if more boy babies die before they are born or right after, there still are more boys than girls among the new babies.

Nature may be very smart in seeing to it that some extra boys are brought into the world. At least, girls may think so, because, for one thing, when they go to a party or a dance, they'll be more likely to have a partner.

## Can't Parents Have Boys or Girls As They Wish?

Parents like to have both girls and boys in their families. When one child has been a boy, parents usually would like the next to be a girl. Or if a girl has come first, they may want the next baby to be a boy. You may be wondering, then, whether there isn't some way by which parents can fix it so a baby will be of the sex they wish. Perhaps you yourself are thinking, "When I get married, I want to have so many girls and so many boys."

Some day—even by the time you are ready to be a parent—scientists may find out how to make this possible. But so far no way is yet known by which parents can have a baby (or their next baby) of the sex they prefer. It is still all a matter of chance, as when tossing up a penny. A coin may come up either heads or tails. So every time there is a race of "boy-making" sperms and "girl-making" sperms to get to an egg, no one can tell which kind of sperm will win. Even if parents have had three or four boys in a row, their next child may still be another boy; or if they have had three or four girls, the next child may again be a girl.

Usually when parents have a lot of children some are boys and some are girls. But there are cases of very large families with eight, nine, ten or more children all of the same sex. This could still be a matter of chance, as when, in tossing up a coin many times, it may be possible to get a succession of heads or a succession of tails. However, it is believed that in such cases heredity may have something to do with it.

There may be more fun being in a family with both boys and girls. If that isn't the way it turns out, though, there often can be advantages in having a lot of sisters (if you are a girl) or a lot of brothers (if you are a boy). In any case, you can be sure that parents love their children just as much if they are boys or if they are girls.

# 6
# WHY YOU LOOK LIKE YOU

You may often have thought about how you got your looks, and why you don't look exactly like anyone else. Also, if you have a brother or a sister, you may have wondered why you look alike in some ways, and quite different in other ways.

Sometimes two children in a family, of different ages, are so much alike that when you see them in school for the first time, you know almost at once that they are related. Perhaps it has happened to you that someone whom you never met before has said, "Aren't you the brother of ——?" or "Aren't you the sister of ——?"

But sometimes one brother can have very dark hair, and another can have light, blond hair, or red hair. One sister can have brown eyes, another blue eyes. Sometimes one child in a family looks so different from another you would never dream they were related. How can this be?

Another question is why one child may look

more like the father, another child more like the mother. Or why, sometimes, a child may hardly resemble either parent at all. In the old days when this happened people often worried that the child had been "changed in the cradle" with someone else's baby. (Haven't you read stories like that?) But now we know it is quite possible for a child to look quite different from the parents and still be as much their own child as one who looks very much like them. The explanation for all such questions will be found in the genes a child inherits.

## *The Look Genes*

In Chapter 3 we learned that among the thousands of genes which came to you from your parents, there were many which were concerned with making your looks: "painter" genes, "sculptor" genes, "hairdresser" genes, and other special kinds of genes for shaping every part of your face and body. We also told how, just as real-life painters, sculptors or other workers may differ in what they do, the genes, too, may differ. One "painter" gene may work to make eyes brown, another may produce blue eyes. Some "sculptor" genes may make a nose short and broad, others may make a nose long and narrow. Some genes may make thin lips, other genes may make full, round lips.

The reason there are so many different colors of eyes, hair and skins, and so many shapes of noses, ears and mouths, is that there are a great many different kinds of genes for people's looks. With animals such as purebred dogs, one can pretty well guess what the young ones will look like. That is because the parents themselves look much the same, having been bred to have much the same kind of "look" genes. But in human beings, who were never bred in any special way, a father and mother are often very different in their looks, and each parent may carry a mixture of genes of many kinds. So their children's looks may be mixed.

It is especially important to know that a parent does not pass on to a child all of his or her kinds of chromosomes and their genes. Only half of the father's 46 kinds of chromosomes—or 23—are passed on to a child, and only half of the mother's 46 chromosomes—another 23. Why this is so may not be hard to guess. For if you had received all of your father's assortment of chromosomes, and all of your mother's, you would have started off with twice as many chromosomes as either of your parents had. Then when some day you married and had a child, that child would in the same way get still another doubled number of chromosomes;

## 44 · WHY YOU ARE YOU

and in a grandchild of yours, the chromosomes would be doubled once again (making 368 chromosomes, if you've been figuring it out). That would get to be pretty crazy if it kept up, and the chromosomes and genes would go crazy, too.

So Nature has cleverly seen to it that each parent gives a child only a half set of chromosomes. That is, each sperm from the father is formed so as to carry only half of his kinds of chromosomes, and each egg from the mother carries only half of her kinds of chromosomes. The two half sets coming together make the full set of

### HOW YOUR PARENTS PASSED ON THEIR CHROMOSOMES TO YOU

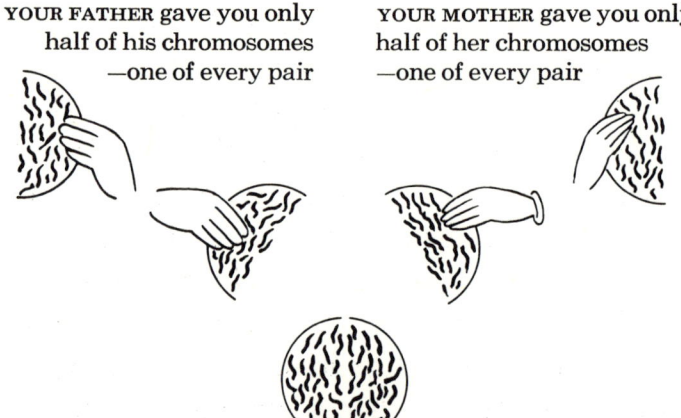

YOUR FATHER gave you only half of his chromosomes —one of every pair

YOUR MOTHER gave you only half of her chromosomes —one of every pair

So, like your parents, you carry two of each kind of chromosomes and their genes

chromosomes and their genes which a child needs —no more and no less.

You may have been thinking: If a parent gives half of his or her chromosomes to one child, and again half to another child, how could there be any chromosomes left for any more children? The answer is that the father and mother can produce any number of copies of their chromosomes. It is in a way like manufacturers of playing cards, who can produce millions of packs of the same cards.

If you continued to think of chromosomes as playing cards, each parent would have a great many decks of 46 chromosomes, made up of 23 pairs, each pair different from the other pairs. The father would then deal out to a child half of a deck of his chromosomes—one chromosome from each of his 23 pairs. The mother would also then deal out half of a deck of her chromosomes, or one chromosome from each of her 23 pairs. That would give the child the full deck, or set of 46 chromosomes, that would be needed.

Is there any rule about which of a parent's chromosomes and their genes a child gets? No. It is all a matter of chance, just as it would be with cards that are shuffled and dealt out. One cannot tell which of a parent's chromosomes a child may get, or which ones the child will not get. What is

## 46 · WHY YOU ARE YOU

certain only—through another wonderful system which nature has worked out—is that a child will get one of every pair of each parent's 23 kinds of chromosomes. (That is, with the exception of the father's pair of "sex" chromosomes. As mentioned in the last chapter, a child can get either the X, to make a girl, or the Y, to make a boy.)

The new assortment of chromosomes which every child receives may be different in a great many ways from the assortment which the father alone has, or the mother alone has. Thus, a child

### WHY CHILDREN IN A FAMILY CAN LOOK SO DIFFERENT

1. If the flower seeds in a package are mixed—

2. Flowers of different colors will grow from them

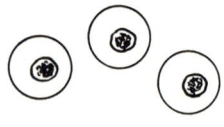

3. If parents have mixed genes in their "seed packages"—

4. Their children may be different in hair and eye colors, faces, etc.

WHY YOU LOOK LIKE YOU · 47

can be different in heredity in many ways, and look different, from either the father or the mother. Also, each child in a family may get an assortment of chromosomes and their genes different from those received by other children. One child could get "brown-eye" genes, another "blue-eye" genes, and so on with many other "look" genes. On the other hand, two of the children in a family could get many of the same "look" genes, and so look more like each other than like a brother or sister who got fewer of the same genes.

### *Guessing About Parents' Genes*

Can't one tell by looking at parents what kind of "look" genes they carry, and so what their children will look like? Sometimes, but not always.

THE "HIDDEN" (RECESSIVE) GENES

Genes for light hair and light eyes may be hiding in parents with dark hair and dark eyes

When both parents pass on the hidden genes, their child may have light hair and light eyes

That is because many genes "hide" in people, or are kept from working by other stronger genes. The blue-eye gene usually acts like that if it is in a person who also has a dark-eye gene. So when parents have dark eyes, one cannot be sure that they are not also carrying hidden blue-eye genes. One finds this out only if dark-eyed parents have children with light-colored eyes. You probably know of cases like that.

When a gene remains hidden in a person it is called a *recessive* gene (meaning one which recedes, or draws back). A gene which can keep another one from working, but does its own work instead, is called a *dominant* gene. For instance, the blue-eye gene is recessive, and the dark-eye gene is dominant. If a child gets a blue-eye gene from one parent, and a dark-eye gene from the other parent, the blue-eye gene will hold back and the dominant, dark-eye gene will cause the child to have dark eyes. But if each parent gives the child a blue-eye gene, and there is no dominant, dark-eye gene to interfere, the two recessive blue-eye genes will work to produce blue eyes.

There also are genes which are only partly dominant, or partly recessive. How the different genes work to produce the many inherited traits in people will be told in the following chapters.

# 7

# YOUR COLORING

Human beings are not nearly as different in natural coloring as are many lower animals, birds or fish.

There is a reason why the differences in coloring between one person and another cannot be so great. It is because all the coloring in all human beings—in their eyes, hair and skin—is produced in much the same way and with almost the same coloring matter. Even though some human eyes may look blue, and others green, gray, brown or black, all have the same kind of brown coloring matter in them. It is just a question of *how much*.

When eyes are as chockful of the brownish coloring matter as they can be, they look black. Where there is less of the color, they look brown. What about "blue" eyes? Here we have a surprise. There is no blue coloring matter in blue eyes, any more than there is blue paint in the sky. What makes the sky look blue is the way the light plays on the dust particles in the air. (At sunset, for instance, when the light changes, you can see lots of other colors in the sky; and when there is a rainbow, you can see bands of brilliant colors, for reasons which you've perhaps already learned in school.) So if you have blue eyes, it is the way they look when the light plays on the little particles of brown color inside the round, central part of your eye called the *iris*.

Green eyes are almost like blue eyes, except that they have a little added yellowish color in them, which, mixed with the "blue" look, makes them look green. (As you probably know, the ocean often looks green when the blue reflection from the sky plays on the yellowish tone of the seawater, caused by particles of sand.)

You should now be able to make some guesses about your own "eye-color" genes. If you have black or very dark brown eyes, you are carrying at least one dark-eye gene which you got from a parent who was probably very dark-eyed; and if your other parent is also dark-eyed, you probably have two dark-eye genes.

If you have blue eyes, you know you are carrying two blue-eye genes. (If you had one dark-eye gene, it would have dominated the blue-eye gene and made your eyes dark.) You know also that a blue-eye gene must have come from each of your parents. They might both be blue-eyed themselves; or one could be blue-eyed and the other dark-eyed but carrying a hidden dark-eye gene; or both of your parents could be dark-eyed, and each could be carrying a hidden blue-eye gene. It is the same with green eyes or gray eyes, the genes for which are also dominated by the dark-eye gene.

With these facts about how the eye-color genes work, it may be fun figuring out which of the genes your parents may be carrying, and which genes they may have passed on to each of any brothers or sisters you may have.

### *Your Hair Color*

Human hair color is produced in almost the same way as is eye color—mainly by the amount of a brownish coloring substance (much like that going into eyes) which hair-coloring genes put into the person's hair.

Each hair, as seen greatly magnified under a microscope, looks like a very long, thin plastic tube. When the brownish coloring substance put in by the genes is very sparse, the hair looks blond,

# HUMAN COLORING

All human coloring is produced in almost the same way: mainly by how much or how little of a certain brownish pigment substance (melanin) goes into the eyes, hair or skin

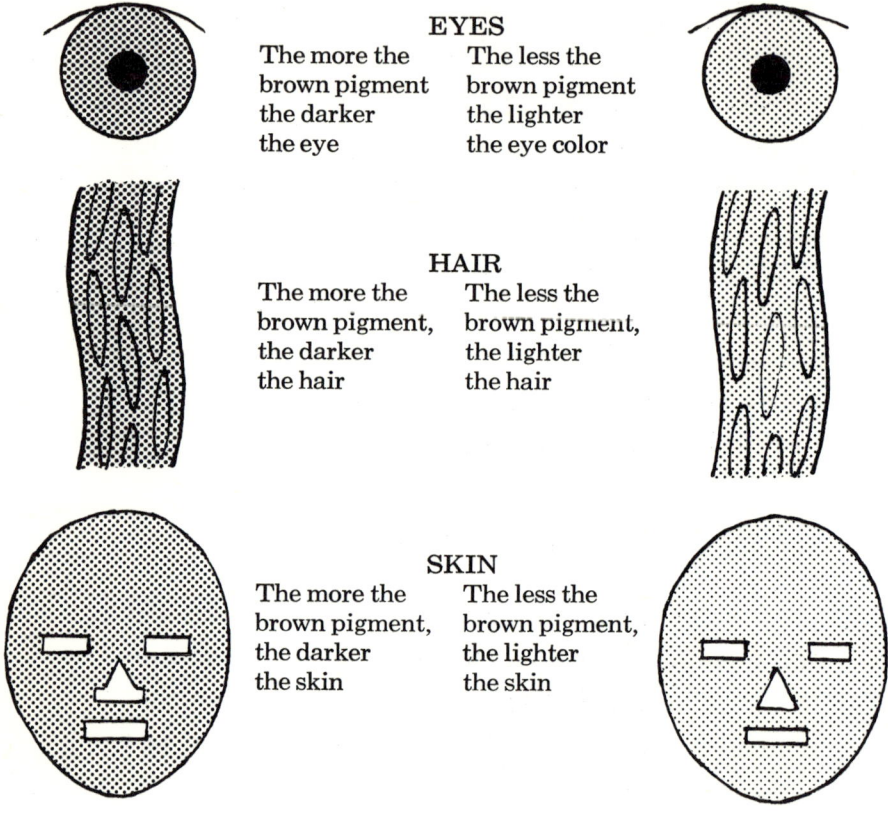

### EYES
The more the brown pigment the darker the eye

The less the brown pigment the lighter the eye color

### HAIR
The more the brown pigment, the darker the hair

The less the brown pigment, the lighter the hair

### SKIN
The more the brown pigment, the darker the skin

The less the brown pigment, the lighter the skin

(For special eye, hair and skin colors, see text)

or yellow. When the genes work to put in more of the brownish substance, the hair looks brown. And when the genes are very active and pack a great deal of the coloring into the hair, the hair looks black. In an opposite way, there are genes which are so weak they produce almost no coloring substance, and so the hair looks white. (Sometimes such genes are found in younger people. In older persons, hair-color genes of any kind tend to become weaker in their action, causing hair to turn gray or white with age.)

"Redheads" have special genes which add to their hair a certain reddish coloring substance, and this shows up if there is not too much brown coloring matter to hide it. Usually two redheaded parents have redheaded children. But sometimes very dark-haired parents may both be carrying hidden "red-hair" genes, so they, too, can have redheaded children.

As with the dark and light eye-color genes, the darker hair-color genes are stronger and *dominant*. The lighter hair-color genes are *recessive*. Thus, if a person has just one dark-hair gene, his hair will be dark. To have light-colored hair, one must have only light-hair genes. You know, therefore, that if you have blond hair you are not carrying any dark-hair gene. But if you have dark hair, you could still be carrying a hidden light-hair gene. This could have come to you if one of your parents has *natural* light-colored hair (bleached hair doesn't count!). Even if both parents are dark-haired, one or the other could be carrying a hidden light-hair gene, and have given it to you.

## *Your Skin Color*

One hears it said that people have "white" skins, or "black" skins, or "yellow" skins, or "red" skins. Actually, no human skins are of these colors. No skin called "white" is like the white paper on this page. (If it were, the person would look like a ghost.) No skin called "black" is really black, like black paint. No skin called "yellow" is really yellow, as is a lemon. And no skin called "red" is really red, like an apple, or the red stripes on a flag. Look at your own skin in the mirror, and see how it compares with anything white, black, yellow or red.

All human skins are mainly different shades of brown. That is because all human skins have the same kind of brown coloring matter in them. As with eye colors and hair colors, it is a question of *how much*.

"White" skin is usually very light brown (except when it's tanned), with a pinkish tone that comes from the blood vessels beneath. "Black" skins have a great deal of the brown coloring matter in them, just as with black eyes or black hair. "Yellow" skins are really brown skins with a little added reddish-yellow substance. American Indians may have in their skins an extra amount of this reddish-yellow substance. But even that doesn't make their skins truly red, even though they were called Redskins by the first explorers who saw them.

To produce the many different shades and kinds of human skin color there are many different genes. Each parent gives a child not one, but a number of "skin-color" genes. Usually, when the skin colors of the two parents are much alike, the colors of their children's skins will be about the same. But if the skin colors of the two parents differ considerably, or if they carry hidden genes of different kinds, children in a family may get various assortments of skin-color genes. One child may therefore have a skin color lighter or darker, or pinker or creamier or yellower, than another.

However, one's skin color need have nothing at all to do with other inherited traits. It is the same with differences in eye color, or hair color. As a popular saying goes, "You can't tell what's in a package by the color of the wrapping."

# 8
# YOUR FACE AND FEATURES

The way in which you may seem to be most different from anyone else in the world—at least in what makes you most easily recognized—is in your face. One reason would be that no one else is ever likely to have your particular mixture of the "feature" genes which shape all parts of your face. Some people may have a nose much like yours, or a mouth, or eyes like yours. But when all the many details of your face are taken together, no other person would have your whole exact combination.

Another reason no one else would look exactly like you, even with the same genes (as in the case of identical twins, whom we'll talk about in a later chapter), is that different things happen to change people's looks from the way their genes had planned them to be. Accidents or sicknesses, how children grow, and what they eat and how they live, can have effects on the shapes of the eyes, the nose, the mouth and the face as a whole. Since no two people have all the same things happening to them, their features will not develop exactly in the same way, no matter what "feature" genes they carry.

One may hear it said that a child has "his father's eyes," "his mother's mouth," "his grandfather's chin," and so on. Have you been told that about one or another of your own features? It may mean only that some "feature" genes you received were the same and worked in the same way as those of the particular parent or grandparent.

For making every part of your face, you got certain genes from both your father and mother. How can it happen, then, that you may have a nose, or eyes, or some other feature, like that of only one of your parents? The explanation—as was said about your eye color or hair color—is that when there are several kinds of genes for the same job, sometimes the gene or genes from one parent will act "bossy" and *dominate* the gene or genes from the other parent. For instance, the "cheek" gene that produces dimples is the dominant kind. If one parent has dimples and the other parent hasn't, the child will very likely have dimples. Other genes which usually are dominant—so that the trait can come from the parent who has it—are those for long lashes, large eyes and big chins.

Some of the "nose" genes are dominant, too.

# HOW THE "LOOK" GENES WORK

## NOSE GENES

Some push the tip of the nose up, some down; some make the nose long, some make it short

Some genes pull the nostrils out, some push them in, to make nose broad or narrow

## EAR GENES

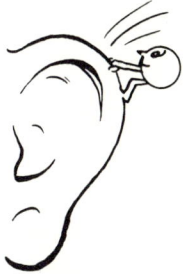
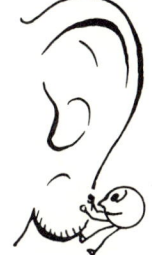

Some make the ears stick out

Some push ear lobes close to the cheek

Some pull ear lobes away from the cheek

## THE "HAIRDRESSER" GENES

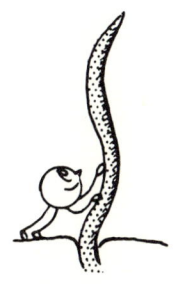

Some make the hair grow out straight

Some make the hair grow out wavy

Some make the hair grow out curly

This is generally true of the genes for the more prominent noses—the bigger or broader or longer ones. But often a parent who has such genes may also carry some other kinds of "nose" genes which are recessive (or hiding). So one child who gets the dominant genes may have a nose like that of the parent with the same kind of nose, while another child, who doesn't get those genes, may have a different kind of nose, or one that is more like that of the other parent. Again, if dominant "nose" genes have come down from a grandparent, a child's nose may be like that grandparent's. However, noses are usually shaped by a number of genes working on different parts (the bridge, nostrils, tip, etc.). So parts of the noses of two persons in a family may be the same and parts may be different.

What has been said about noses also applies to shapes of mouths, ears and eyes, where dominant and recessive genes, or combinations of genes, could produce resemblances or differences between you and one parent or another, or between you and a sister or brother.

### The "Hairdresser" Genes

People have been doing so many things with their hair, or can change their hair shapes and

YOUR FACE AND FEATURES · 61

styles in so many ways if they wish, that perhaps the kind of hair one was born to have may no longer seem as important as it once was. Just the same, you may want to know how your natural hair shape came to be what it is.

Is your hair naturally straight? Wavy? Curly? Tightly curled or woolly? Whichever way it is shaped is because of how your "hairdresser" genes have made the hair grow out of the scalp.

Through a microscope each hair, greatly magnified, looks like a very long, thin tube (as we said when we talked about coloring), or a very thin, flexible pipe. If a straight hair were cut across, you could see it was very round. That's why it can come up or lie stiff and straight. A wavy hair, cut across, is more flattened, or oval, which makes it twist, or wave more, as it grows out. A curly hair is still flatter, so it is more likely to curl, like a ribbon. And very curly, or woolly, hair is the most flattened; further, this kind of hair often tends to twist up in little bunches close to the scalp. Hair also grows in different thicknesses, some people having very thick hair, and some thin hair.

For each kind of hair there are different genes. Some of these genes are dominant, some are recessive. Different combinations of the "hairdresser" genes will explain why straight hair, wavy hair and curly hair may often be found in the same family. Usually if both parents have straight hair, all the children have straight hair. If one or both parents have curly or wavy hair, the children will probably have the same kind of hair, but a child with straight hair is possible. If either parent's hair is of the very curly, woolly type (or the thick, black, straight type) a child's hair is most likely to be the same as that parent's.

But, as we said, a person's hair form nowadays need not depend just on the genes. A girl with straight hair may make her hair wavy or curly, if she wishes, by using curlers or hair-sets. And a girl with very curly hair may straighten it out. Needless to say, this won't change the genes. Whatever one does to one's hair, the genes will cause the new hair growing out to be just as it was before. However, curly hair tends to get less curly as a child grows older, and wavy hair later may become almost straight.

### *Other Features*

Mouths and lips come in many different shapes. Some lips look very thick, and others very thin. But the difference may be mostly in the way lips are turned out or turned in. If your own lips are not thick, stand in front of a mirror and turn up your upper lip with your fingers, and next do the same with your lower lip. You will see how your lips can be made to look thick, too. Of course, this turning out is done naturally by the "lip" genes which some people inherit—mainly those who are of the Negro, or black, race.

How different mouths look may also depend a lot on the teeth inside. Various shapes and sizes of teeth can be inherited, and sometimes a peculiarity in certain teeth (such as the front teeth sticking out) will be found in a family. You may want to compare your own teeth with those of your parents, and with any brothers or sisters you have, to see if there is some special kind of "tooth" resemblance. However, the way people talk, eat and use their mouths may also affect the shapes of their teeth and mouths. When a child is growing up and the teeth and mouth are being developed, it is especially important to be careful about any habits which may affect their later appearance.

*Eye shapes* aren't too often given much attention, but there are inherited differences in them which may strongly affect people's looks. If your eyes are larger or smaller than average, or if they are farther apart or closer together than in most people, or are straight across or slanted, this would probably be due to the way your genes worked.

*Ear shapes* may be the least noticed of a person's features (especially in girls who cover them up with their hair—or in some boys who do, too). But there are many little differences in ear shapes which are inherited. One such difference which you may find if you look is that in some ears the *lobe*—the lower soft part of the ear—is attached to the side of the face, while in other ears the lobe is free and separated from the face. (What kind of ear lobe do you have and do others in your family have?) Also inherited may be sizes of ears, and whether they are close to the head or push out a good ways.

### *How Your Face May Change*

You will already have seen, as you've been growing, how much your face has changed since you were very young. The change from year to year may not have been too great. But sometimes—especially during the big growing-up period called *puberty* or *adolescence*—a face may change so much that friends or relatives who haven't seen a boy or a girl for a long while may hardly recognize him or her. (This may have happened to you.)

Among the natural changes that may occur

during or after puberty are those in eye and hair color. When eyes in a child are light in color, they may become a little darker. Hair that is blond, or light brown or light red, may also darken a little. The shape of the hair often changes, too. Hair that is curly may become less so, and if it is wavy, it may become a little straighter. (Of course, with girls there is no way of telling what their hair color or hair shape will be, once they begin going to beauty parlors.)

One thing to remember is that your "look" genes are always there. But they may do new or different things at different points in your life. In fact, they are responsible for many of the changes already made in your looks, and for some still to be made. Many "look" genes, like other genes, have a time schedule. At certain stages or ages they may speed up or slow down their work, and sometimes a gene which has been "asleep" may suddenly spring into action.

Another interesting fact is that your "face" genes may in time make you look more like your parents (or at least one of them) or like some brother and sister, than you do now. In other words, family resemblances often grow greater as people get older. This is especially likely to happen if members of the family go on living together, in the same way. For another thing to keep in mind is that your looks will always be affected by your health, by what and how much you eat, by how you take care of yourself, by many of your habits and by the way you use and work the muscles of your face.

# 9

# YOUR BODY

If you are nearing the teen ages (thirteen and after), or are already in them, your body is undergoing some of the most interesting and important changes of your life.

During this period—of puberty or adolescence—the changes that can be seen most quickly and easily are, of course, in size. You find (or have found) yourself shooting up amazingly, and putting on weight at the same time. But a big difference also begins to show itself when puberty comes, usually much earlier in girls than in boys.

When children are very little, and both boys and girls wear diapers or jumpers, one cannot see much difference between their bodies. This reminds me of what happened one day when I was walking with a young niece of mine, and we saw a woman friend with a twin-baby carriage coming toward us. We had heard that she had had twin babies, and that they were a boy and a girl. One was named Johnny and the other Jennie.

"Can you tell which is which?" I asked my niece as we looked into the carriage.

"Oh, that's easy," she replied. "The one dressed in blue is the boy, and the one in pink is the girl!"

The mother of the twins burst out laughing. "I'm so sorry," she said. "I didn't mean to play a trick on anyone, but I was dressing the twins in a hurry, and put the pink clothes on Johnny and the blue clothes on Jennie!"

Perhaps parents dress boy and girl babies in different colors because if it weren't for the sex organs it might be hard to tell them apart. (But why blue is picked for boys and pink for girls nobody seems to know.) Even when boys and girls are five or six, it often is hard to see much difference in the rest of their bodies. If they were dressed in the same clothes and had their hair cut the same way, you could make many mistakes in trying to tell them apart. Just the same, there are many differences in their bodies, which result from the different actions of their sex chromosomes, as explained in Chapter 5.

Boy babies usually are just a little bigger and heavier than girl babies. The bones in little boys are also a little heavier and thicker than those of girls. The muscles of boys are a little more developed. As boys begin to run around and exercise more than girls, this helps to make them stronger. The older boys grow to be, the greater usually becomes the difference in strength between them and girls. Remember, though, we are talking about *most* boys and girls—not *all*. Many times a boy finds a girl his own age is stronger than he.

The really big differences between boys and girls come with the puberty changes. The first thing noticed is that girls have a considerable head start over boys in their growth. That is, girls usually begin to shoot up in height, and their bodies

THE BOY-GIRL "GROWING SEE-SAW"

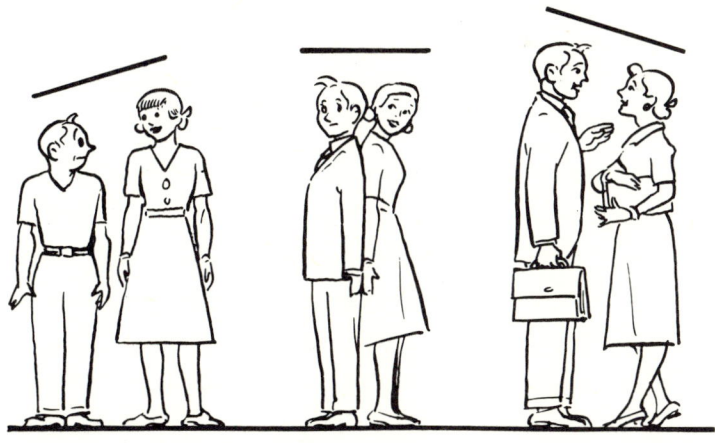

First, girls taller    Then both even    Then boys taller

begin to develop toward the mature, womanly form, when they are eleven, twelve or thirteen. With boys, the puberty changes may not come until a year or two later. For a while, then, a girl may be taller and heavier than most of the boys her age. But after boys catch up, they tend to be taller by four or five inches—or more—and heavier by many pounds.

## *How Tall Will You Be?*

What decides the height which you will reach when full grown depends mainly on your "growth" genes. As a human being, your genes set limits on both how tall and how short you can be. A mouse can grow only so big; a cat can grow so big; an elephant or a hippopotamus can grow very big; and a whale—the biggest of all animals—can grow to be eighty or ninety feet long.

Human beings (taking women and men together) usually range in height between five and six feet. Some people may be smaller, and some larger. But there are no such great differences in size between people as there are between dogs—a tiny toy poodle and a huge St. Bernard, for instance—who have been bred to be as different in size as possible.

In your own case, you can probably tell by looking at your parents and other close relatives what kind of growth genes you may be carrying, and about how tall you can expect to be. Usually when a father is tall and the mother is quite tall for a woman, every child in the family grows to be tall. If both parents are short, it is still possible for a child to be tall, especially if there were some tall people in the parents' families. Often in these cases the children are mixed in height, some short, some tall. You must keep in mind, though, that the same "tallness" genes work differently in boys and girls, and that while a boy may get the same growth genes from his parents as his sister, he may grow to be four, five or six inches taller.

But something else besides the genes decides how tall people will be. You may have noticed that in the United States and most other advanced countries, children today usually grow to be taller than their parents, and often much taller than their grandparents were. The reason is that young people now are having better food, care and medical attention, which improves their health and helps to increase their growth. This is easy to understand if you know something about gardening or farming. When plants are in good soil, and have plenty of rain and sunshine, and no sicknesses or troubles such as blights, bugs or worms, they grow taller and bigger than do plants that have less favorable conditions. People are not very different from plants in that way.

Years ago the *environments*—which include all the living conditions—were not nearly as good as they are now, and so people did not grow to be as tall. For instance, the knights of old were usually very short—often just "shrimps" compared to today's soldiers—as you can see in any museum which exhibits the armor they wore. Many of today's parents, too, when they were young, did not have as good food or as healthy conditions as their children now have, so their sons and daughters are growing to be taller than they are. However, in many places inside the United States and in other countries, children are still living in bad environments, with not enough good food, vitamins or proper care. So even if they have good growth genes, these are not able to work as well as they could under better conditions.

But why, in the same family, does one boy grow to be taller than another, or one girl taller than her sisters (or even than a brother, sometimes)? For several reasons: Just as children in a family may get different genes for eye color, hair color or other features, they may get different kinds of growth genes. There may also be differences in health, as when one child has a disease which interferes with his growth. Other reasons may be differences in what and how much children eat and how food is used in their bodies; or in the amount of exercise one child has as compared with another.

One must also remember that young people do not all begin their big growth at the same age, and may not grow at the same rate. One boy or girl may begin to shoot up before another, and for a while may be several inches taller. When the shorter boy or girl starts to grow, he or she sometimes becomes the tallest after a few years. You may not be able to tell for certain how tall you are likely to be until you are about sixteen or seventeen. Many girls continue to grow until they are twenty, and some boys until twenty-two or twenty-three.

Anyway, you will probably be tall enough. There really are just a few inches between people we call "tall" and those we call "short." What is more, shortness need not stop a girl from having plenty of beaus, or a boy from having plenty of girl friends, or either from doing well in school and being successful in jobs. Many of our most famous men have been shorties. What is important is not how big you are on the outside, but how big a person you are inside of you.

## *Your Body Form*

One of the biggest differences which develop between boys and girls at puberty is in the shapes of their bodies.

In girls the bodies become fuller and curvier, while in boys the bodies become harder and more muscular. The hips in girls grow wider, while in boys the hips are narrower in proportion, and the shoulders become much broader and squarer. The arms and legs of boys also grow longer in proportion to their bodies than do those of girls.

The difference that can be seen most easily is in *breasts*. A girl's breasts become much bigger, fuller and softer, whereas the breasts in boys remain almost flat. In some girls the breasts grow bigger than in others. Often the size of the girl may not matter. One girl may be shorter and thinner than another and yet have larger breasts. The sizes and shapes of breasts sometimes run in families, so it is quite possible a girl may have breasts like her mother's when she was young.

In a boy the biggest changes which occur while he grows taller and heavier are in his bones and muscles. The bones become longer and thicker; the muscles in the arms and legs, and all over his body, become larger and stronger. Of course, the more a boy exercises and takes part in athletics, the more his muscles will develop. But he does not have to be an athlete in order to become well-developed. Just an average amount of exercise, and sensible eating and habits, will enable him to become a fully mature man.

Going with a boy's bigger muscles, there is one other easily noticed sex difference which comes at puberty: the growth of *beards* in boys (and aren't girls glad it does *not* happen to them!). While girls also have hair on their faces, it is much finer and lighter, and harder to see, than the hair that grows on the sides of the face, the upper lip, and the jaws and chin of boys.

Boys also develop much more hair on their chests and arms than girls do. But having a lot of hair on the chest, or having little, doesn't mean anything with regard to how "manly" a boy is. In some families the men are very hairy, in other families not. Often a boy can guess by looking at his father how hairy he himself is going to be. As a rule, men of the white race have more hair on their faces and bodies than Negroes, and those with the least hair on their faces or bodies are Chinese, Japanese and American Indians, who all belong to the same Mongoloid race.

Overweight is a cause of worry to many young

people. It may develop during the puberty period when various changes take place too rapidly in the person's system and eating habits. Often the fat girl or boy has an appetite that can't be controlled, especially when it comes to candy, cake and other fattening foods. However, there are many cases where the habits of the much overweight person are not to blame, the cause being some disorder in the glands or other chemical workings which interfere with the proper use of food, so that too much of what is eaten is converted into fat that stays in the body. Some of the conditions which produce extreme overweight may be due to heredity. Where the urge to overeat is due mainly to puberty changes or to something in the person's mind, the "fatty" often slims down a lot during the next few years. Some girls who were pretty plump in their childhood or early teens become beauty queens later.

So far we have talked about the *outside* of your body and the changes and differences in the bodies of boys and girls. Now we turn to look at the *insides*, where we will find some of the reasons for these changes and differences, and other facts to explain what your body does and how it does it.

# 10

# YOUR "MACHINERY" AND "CHEMICAL FACTORY"

A spaceship flying to the moon is a wonderful machine. So is a color TV; a giant telescope, which can see stars billions of miles away; a huge printing press turning out hundreds of big newspapers a minute; and all sorts of other machines you may know about which do amazing things.

But there is no more marvelous machine than your own body. In fact, you are made up of dozens of "machines" both on the inside and outside of you. Any one of these is more remarkable than any of the most complex machines which human beings themselves have been able to manufacture. Of course, these machines of yours do not have wheels or springs or electrical parts. They are made of flesh, blood, muscles and bones which are *alive*. That is why a more proper name for them is *living mechanisms*. But in what they do, they work much like machines.

Your hands pick up and manipulate objects; your eyes are like TV cameras that are constantly taking and showing you pictures; your legs and feet are mechanisms which move you about; your ears are "telephone" receivers; your heart is a pump; your lungs are "air conditioners"; and your brain is a "thinking machine," more complicated and wonderful than are any of the giant computers that are in use today.

But the biggest and most marvelous job done by all of your body's machines working together is to make you a *human being*, and not an animal. Actually, human beings are animals, too, but different from any other animals. Scientists therefore speak of people as "higher" animals, and of monkeys, cats, dogs, elephants, birds, fish, insects and all other living creatures as "lower" animals. However, to make things simpler, we will often use the word "animals" to mean only the lower ones.

## *You And The Animals*

When you go to a zoo, or you live on a farm, you can recognize many ways in which your "machinery" is different from that of the lower animals.

No other animal has hands like yours, which are so nimble and able to do so many things. Look at the paws of cats or dogs. They have no fingers, and could not possibly pick up and hold objects with them, or work with tools. The hoofs of horses and cows are even more useless than paws when it comes to doing anything with them. What about monkeys and apes, who are the animals most like people? Don't they have hands pretty much like yours? Not quite. Their thumbs are very short, and their fingers aren't as flexible. Next time you watch them on TV or in a zoo, notice how much clumsier their hands are than yours.

One of the biggest physical advantages human beings have is their ability to stand up straight on their legs, and to walk or run erect. No other animal can do this. Chimpanzees and gorillas come closest to walking the way people do, but you will notice that their legs are very short, and the best they can do is walk for short distances in a twisting, clumsy way, like babies. Usually they soon bend over and help themselves along with their hands, the knuckles pushing the ground. The fact that human beings do not have to walk on all fours makes possible an even greater advantage: their hands are left free to work with, which has enabled them to make and use tools as no other

# YOU AND THE ANIMALS

## Much of your "machinery" is better than any animal's

Most animals can't see colors. To them red, white and blue are just gray, white and gray.

No animal can walk or dance in the way you can

No animal has fingers as flexible as yours

Even where animals do have advantages, you can still beat them with the use of man-made machines

animal could do, no matter how smart he was.

Your eyes also are different from those of most animals. You cannot see in the dark as many of them do. But you can see something they cannot: you can see colors of every kind. Except for apes and monkeys, all other animals—including dogs, cats and birds—are color-blind for the most part. They see colors mainly as lighter or darker shades of gray and black, about the way you see things in black-and-white movies and TV pictures. Human eyes are set on the same plane (on a straight line across the face) whereas most animals have eyes set at an angle on opposite sides of the head. Your eyes can *focus* together—both looking at numerous things at the same time—enabling you to see in depth. In animals whose eyes are on opposite sides of the head (like horses, dogs or cats) the eyes work individually, but see things more flatly than do human eyes.

## *Animal's Advantages*

You would not expect to have everything about you better than lower animals have. Each animal needs some special kind of equipment so that it can do all the things it must to live. Birds have wings. Fish have fins and breathing equipment for living in the water. Polar bears have thick furs. Deer have fast-moving legs. In the same way, almost any animal may have certain equipment which is different from and better than your own. But if there is anything people lack in their bodies, they do have one tremendous advantage. They are able to make machines or equipment with which they can do almost everything any animal can do, and better. You can move much faster than a deer, a leopard or a rabbit by getting in an automobile or hopping onto a motorcycle. You can fly faster and farther than any bird when you are in an airplane (not to mention what you could do in a space capsule). You can swim under water with aqualungs, and you can stay under water for many days in a submarine.

Another special thing your human body machinery enables you to do is to live any place you wish in the world—in the hottest climates or the coldest ones. Animals of each kind can live only in the places for which nature has designed them, unless they are kept under special conditions by human beings in zoos or in homes. Tropical birds or tropical fish could not otherwise live where it is very cold. Penguins or polar bears could not live where it is very hot. Some animals have to live in the mountains, some by the seashore. Animals sometimes can change their coverings to fit the seasons up to a point, but not in the way you can change your clothing from one day to the next, or keep yourself comfortable with heaters or air conditioners.

Animals can eat and digest many foods that you could not eat without getting sick. But no animal can eat, taste or appreciate as many different foods as you can, or get as enormous a variety of foods. Nor can any animal cook or prepare raw foods in various ways. A young animal of any kind doesn't have to ask, "Mom, what's for dinner?" He knows. It's just about the same old menu all the time.

### *How Human Beings Are Most Special*

Of all the differences between you and the animals, the most important one, as you can easily guess, is in your "thinking machinery." First, you have more brain for your size than any animal. Notice how big and round the top of your head is above your eyebrows, and how your forehead goes straight up and is not slanted back like a cat's, a dog's, a horse's, or even a chimpanzee's. That is because the top of your head has to be like a box to hold your large brain.

Second, it is not only the bigness of your brain, but the better way it works, that enables you to think better and faster, and to learn more than any animal can. Animals can think, learn and remember only a little. They have to depend mostly on what is called their *instincts*. These are ways of acting and doing things which are born into them; the machinery of their brains and bodies can proceed to do many things that are needed without their having to be taught by their parents or other animals. No one has to teach a bird how to build her particular kind of nest and what to feed her young; or a spider how to spin its web and catch flies; or a beaver how to build a dam; or a bee how to make honey. Each animal is equipped by nature with the ability to do many things in a certain way. The animal may be able to learn a little by experience, but does nothing too new or too different from what the other animals of its kind have always done.

Human beings may also have certain instincts, but they can go far beyond them in their thinking, behavior and what they can do. If you had to depend only on instincts you would act much like a mechanical doll, without knowing what you are doing. You would do everything exactly the way your ancestors had always done it for tens of thousands of years. You would rarely learn anything new. But as a human being with a human brain, there is almost no limit to the new things you can learn, and the way you can be trained or can train yourself to live and work.

## *Talking, Reading, Writing*

Your better brain is not the only reason you are so much smarter than the lower animals. First, you also can talk. That makes it possible to ask questions and get answers, and to exchange conversation and ideas with other people. No animals can talk as you can. They have no "voice machine" like yours, and even if they had, they could not use it as you do. Parrots and certain other birds can be taught to speak a few words, but they don't know what they are saying. Dogs cannot do much more than bark, and cats can't do much more than meow. Even clever chimpanzees can only chatter and grunt, although their noises are a sort of limited language which other chimpanzees can understand.

How does your voice machine work?—and what brings the changes in your voice at puberty? Here is an explanation: Your voice is much like a stringed musical instrument—a uke, a guitar, a violin, a harp or even a piano. In any of these instruments there are short, thin strings to make the high notes, and longer, thicker strings to make the deep, low notes. In the "voice box" inside your throat there are such strings too (called the *vocal chords*), although they are made of flesh. In a young child's throat the voice strings are thin and short, so the sound they make is high. But as you grow, your voice strings become longer and thicker, so your voice becomes deeper and lower.

Why are girls' voices different from those of boys? Because the voice boxes in boys are larger, and their voice strings are longer and thicker. The difference becomes greater as boys grow older, so their voices become deeper and lower. Also, since boys' voices change more during puberty, it may be a little harder for them to get used to their new voices, and so sometimes they go suddenly from high to low, or low to high. But this is only for a short while. In some boys, too, the voice box and vocal chords are so constructed that their voice remain higher, or of the tenor type, while in other boys, with different voice machines, the deeper baritone or bass types of voice may be developed. Among girls, in much the same way, higher and lower ranges of voices are produced— the soprano, alto and contralto.

In addition to being able to speak, another tremendous advantage you have is that you can read and write. In books you can learn what other people have learned through the ages—ever since they found out how to put into writing their thoughts and happenings—and also what the brightest and best-informed writers can tell you today. You, too, can write down what you learn for other people to read. But animals can acquire nothing of what their ancestors may have learned, or leave any records of their knowledge for their descendants.

> *The elephant and the kangaroo*
> *The ostrich and the lark*
>   *Don't know any more than*
>   *Their ancestors did*
> *When they went on Noah's Ark*

So be glad you have the "machinery" that makes you a human being. The more you use that machinery in the best way you can, the less like an animal you will be.

### Your Chemical Factories

We've been talking so far about the parts of your body which work like machinery. There are other

## YOUR "CHEMICAL FACTORIES"

The chart shows the principal organs and glands which produce needed chemicals of your body, and tells what they do. When any of these organs or glands fails to work properly, either because of misbehaving genes or some outside causes, diseases, defects or abnormalities connected with its processes will result.

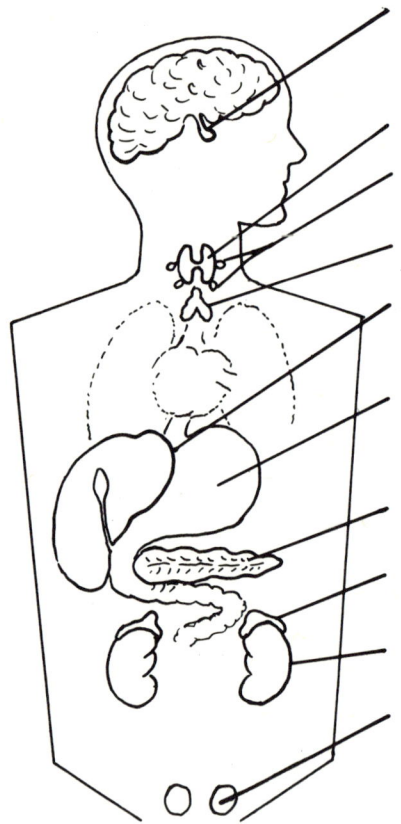

**PITUITARY:** Regulates workings of other glands and the processes of growth and development. Stimulates sex functioning.

**THYROID:** Regulates body chemical processes.

**PARATHYROIDS:** Govern bone formation and help regulate nervous system.

**THYMUS:** Helps fight off disease germs during childhood.

**LIVER:** Secretes bile needed to digest fat, and manufactures or transforms many other chemical substances.

**STOMACH:** Produces some of fluids which prepare food for digestion in intestines, which in turn produce further digestive chemicals.

**PANCREAS:** Secretes insulin which converts starches and regulates use of sugar.

**ADRENALS:** Help regulate nervous system, and affect emotional and sex processes.

**KIDNEYS:** Eliminate waste products. Help maintain blood and fluid circulation.

**SEX GLANDS:** Ovaries in girls, testes in boys. Help to produce sex characteristics and affect the sex processes and functions.

*Note:* Many additional chemicals are produced by cells throughout the body which act as miniature "chemical factories."

parts, inside of you, which are more like chemical factories. In the chemistry laboratory of a school, there are rows and rows of bottles of various chemicals. But your own body produces many more different kinds of chemicals.

Among the chemical factories of your body are the stomach, the liver, the kidneys, the pancreas, the gall bladder and the glands. These manufacture a tremendous variety of chemicals which enable you to digest your food, to produce the material for building your body, to control your growth, to work your muscles, to make your blood, to provide the coloring for your eyes, hair and skin, and to perform many other functions.

In certain ways, also, your chemical factories act like drugstores to fill prescriptions when the needs arise. If disease germs enter your body, some of your chemicals are rushed out to fight them off. When you have sicknesses, one or another of your chemical factories sends out drugs which help to cure you. When you cut yourself, chemicals waiting in your blood hurry to stop the bleeding and heal the wounds. If you break a bone, there are chemicals in you to knit the broken ends together.

Among the most important of your chemicals are the *hormones* (HOR-moans) produced by different glands. One of these glands, the *pituitary* (pit-U-it-ary), is embedded deep inside your head below the center of your brain. While only the size of a bean, it produces a number of different hormones which have powerful effects on many functions of the body and on the workings of other glands, including the *sex glands*.

The sex glands are the ones which differ considerably in males and females. If you are a boy, your sex glands are the *testicles* (or *testes*), contained in the bag of skin called the *scrotum* which hangs behind your penis. If you are a girl, your sex glands are your *ovaries*, inside your body in the lower part of your abdomen.

Both the male's testicles and the female's ovaries produce *sex hormones*. In males, the sex hormones that are mostly produced are called *androgens* (AN-dro-jens). In females the sex hormones mostly produced are called *estrogens* (ESS-tro-jens). The differences in the amounts of each type of sex hormones, which increase as puberty comes on, have a great deal to do with how the bodies of boys develop in one way and those of girls in another way. The growth of beards on the faces of boys, the bigger development of their muscles, the broadening of their shoulders, the deepening of their voices, are the results of their sex hormones working together with other effects of their male "sex" genes. In girls, the development of their breasts, as well as the shaping of other parts of their figures in a mature womanly way, and the development of their sex organs and womb, are a result of their sex hormones working together with their female "sex" genes.

Going with the puberty sex changes, there is also the preparation for boys and girls to become parents some day. In boys the testicles begin to produce the *sperms* we talked about in Chapter 2. In girls their ovaries begin producing eggs in a form which, if they are fertilized by sperms, can develop into babies. The production of these eggs (usually one at a time) also leads to *menstruation*, which occurs in girls about every fourth week or so. This results from the fact that when an egg is produced, the girl's womb prepares itself for the possibility that some day an egg may be fertilized and develop into a baby. So, just as soil is prepared by the farmer for planting, nature prepares the lining of the womb to receive and nourish a fertilized egg. But if the egg is not fertilized by a sperm it will not take root, and so the blood and other material which has been prepared in the womb will be left to flow out of the body.

The sex glands are the only ones which work very differently in boys and girls, and have such different effects. What other glands and other organs do—or are supposed to do—becomes most noticeable when they fail to work properly, or in the usual way. Sometimes this is because of certain genes, and sometimes not. How and why people may be unusual in one way or another will be told in the next chapter.

## 11

# THE UNUSUAL PEOPLE

Look at your hands. Do you have five fingers on each (thumb included)? It may seem like a silly question—unless you happen to be one of those unusual persons (a few in a thousand or more) who was born not with five fingers, but with six, or four, or three. Often where there are extra fingers there also are extra toes, and if there are missing fingers there may be missing toes.

Look again at your own fingers. Does each one have three sections—the tip part (with the fingernail), the middle, and the bottom part? In all probability, yes. But there are some children who are born with only two sections to each finger, the middle section being missing, so that their hands look stubby. Because of that missing middle section, the fingers and hands can't be used as easily and in the same way as those which have all three sections to each finger.

## UNUSUAL EFFECTS OF GENES

Hands may be made with *extra fingers* (or missing fingers)

*"Stub hands"*— middle joints of fingers missing

An *albino:* The "color" genes do not work, so the hair and eyes are without color

A *midget*, a *dwarf* and a *"giant"*—each produced by different types of unusual "growth" genes

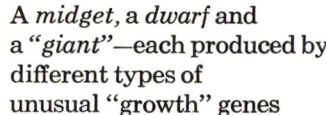

(To see what was written, hold this upside down in front of a mirror)

One of the oddest genes causes a person to read and write upside down and backwards

The hands with extra fingers, missing fingers or missing finger sections are among the unusual types which can be produced by *heredity*. When we talked about *genes*, we said that each of the many thousands of human genes is like a worker with a special job to do. In most human beings, the genes for the same jobs work in very much the same way. The "hand" genes in almost everybody act to produce a thumb and four fingers, with the finger joints and shapes being only slightly different. Likewise, there is not too much difference in how the genes fashion other structural parts of one person as compared with another. If you look at a number of human skeletons you will see how much alike they seem to be.

We sort of take it for granted that each of the genes will do what it is expected to do. But there are genes that don't follow the rules, so once in a while a person is born with a part of the body that is formed differently, or an organ that works differently, from the usual way. Being unusual—or different from the average—may sometimes be good and be considered an advantage. But if it means not being able to work and act as well as most other people, or not being as healthy, it becomes a disadvantage, and may then be spoken of as an *abnormality* (away from the normal).

Let us take the matter of a person's height, for example. The average height of men in the United States now is about 5 feet 9 inches. To be taller than average is regarded by many persons as an advantage. If a young man is over six feet tall, it may help him in various sports. If he gets to be six-feet-six or -eight, or -ten—almost up to seven feet—it may give him a big advantage in basketball, though it may not help him in other ways. This kind of tallness may be in the "normal" range: That is, it can be due to genes that make a man grow taller without keeping him from also being strong and healthy.

But if a man gets to be much over seven feet in height—growing and growing until he is eight feet tall or over—there is probably something wrong with his "growth" gland, the pituitary. As he grows, he may therefore become weaker. An example was a young man in Pennsylvania, who reached the height of 8 feet 10 inches (the tallest of any human being ever known) and was still growing—but becoming steadily weaker—when he died in 1940 at the age of twenty-two.

At the opposite end of extreme tallness is extreme shortness. The shortest (or smallest) human beings are of different kinds. The tiniest are the *midgets*, whose growth glands and genes stop working early in childhood and keep them from reaching beyond 3 feet 6 inches in height. Midget men and women have the same proportions in their heads, bodies and limbs as larger people. They are therefore different from another type of small people, the *dwarfs*, whose shortness comes from unusual genes which causes them to develop with very short, stubby arms and legs, although their trunks are almost normal, and their heads may be oversized. A further difference is that these dwarfs often have children like themselves, whereas midgets seldom have children and are usually born to normal-sized parents.

*Pygmies* are still another kind of short people. They have average proportions, but because of their "shortness" genes, the grown men among them may be no more than 4 feet 6 inches tall. Pygmies are found in Africa, New Guinea, the Philippines and Malaya.

Looking now at details of the body, there is no part, inside or out, no organ and no human "chemical factory," which in some persons is not unusual or abnormal. If an abnormality appears in a child at birth, it is called *congenital* (con-JEN-it-al). There are a great many different congenital abnormalities. Some are due to the failure of this or that gene to work properly, or to something wrong with the inherited chromosomes. Some abnormalities are caused by accidents while the child is developing in the mother, or to something wrong or missing in the food and chemicals that reach the baby in the womb. One cannot always know the cause, nor need the mother be blamed. Also, while certain conditions can be corrected after a child is born, others cannot. (However, the fact that a condition is inherited does not mean nothing can be done about it. Many inherited diseases and defects can be cured, or their effects made less serious.)

Some of the congenital abnormalities affect the senses, or the working parts of the body. You may see the results in children who are blind, or with very poor eyesight; or who are deaf, and so, because they cannot hear sounds, also cannot speak properly; or who have something wrong with their muscles, which interferes with their walking or movements. Defects in the nervous system can cause some children to have epilepsy which shows itself from time to time in convulsions, or strange acts over which they have no control.

*Bone defects* may cause curved spines, or misshapen parts of the body. Some children are born with the conditions called cleft palate or harelip, in which the upper lip and roof of the mouth are not completely formed, so there is a division between them. (Often these conditions can be corrected by an operation.) There also are many skin conditions which can be caused by improperly working genes.

Inside the body there may be defects in the heart, kidneys, stomach and other organs of babies when they are born. Some of these conditions may be due to mistakes of genes, and some to accidents while the babies were developing. (Things that may go wrong with the brains of children will be discussed in a later chapter.)

The "chemical factories" in people may fail to work properly in one way or another, and so be responsible for various conditions. One unusual type of person you can easily recognize is the *albino*. In this person the "coloring" genes fail to produce the needed coloring substances, so the hair looks bleached white (different from ordinary white or blond hair); the eyes look pink, because while there is no coloring in the front part of the eyes, pink shows through from the blood vessels inside. Albino skin looks pale-pinkish for a similar reason. Parents with every kind of skin-color themselves—even Negro or American Indians—sometimes carry hidden "albino" genes. These, coming together, produce albino children. (As you may know, there also are albinos among almost all animals—horses, elephants, dogs, cats, deer, seals, mice, fish and so on—although not all animals which are white are albinos.)

*Blood defects* of many kinds may also be due to something wrong in people's inherited "chemical factories." *Hemophilia* (hee-mo-FEEL-ya) is the "bleeding" condition in which a person's blood lacks the natural substance required to make it clot, and so he is in great danger if he is cut and is not given something at once to stop the bleeding. In other inherited blood diseases, the *anemias* (an-EEM-i-as), not enough red blood cells are produced, or those which are produced are not properly formed, so the person's body does not get the necessary nourishment. In some conditions the blood does not carry certain substances for fighting off infections.

*Allergies* (AL-er-jees) are conditions in which persons' bodies cannot properly handle certain foods or drugs, or certain substances with which they come in contact. The results may be sneezing fits, or breaking out into skin rashes, or digestive upsets. Allergies may be very serious, or they may be only annoying. Almost everyone is allergic to something—to one or another kind of food, fruit, vegetable, drug, chemical, animal fur and just about everything you can name—although different people are allergic to different things. In one case a boy got sneezing fits mysteriously only on Sundays. The mystery was solved when it was found he was allergic to the colored inks in the Sunday comic section. Allergies are sometimes inherited, sometimes not, which may explain why members of a family may have the same kind of allergy, or different allergies.

One of the most interesting facts about diseases and defects is the difference in how boys and girls, or men and women, are affected. People have always thought that girls are more "delicate" than boys. But the opposite is true. While boys have bigger muscles and greater strength, they are much more likely to have something wrong with their bodies; and when boys get sick, it is much more likely to be serious than when girls do. The difference starts even before boys and girls are born.

One reason why many more males than females have certain diseases and defects will be found in the difference in their sex chromosomes. As told in Chapter 5, a girl receives at conception *two* X chromosomes, a boy only one X, plus the little (though powerful) Y chromosome. It happens that the X chromosome is very big, and has hundreds of genes. Among the genes on different X chromosomes there may be some which do not work properly. In a girl, if one of her Xs happens to have this or that bad gene, the chances are very great that her other X will carry a good gene for the job, and so the effects of the bad one will be stopped. But if a boy has a bad gene on his single X, there are no genes in his little Y chromosome to block the effects. So the boy can develop one of the diseases or defects caused by bad X genes. Such conditions are called *sex-linked*.

There are a great number of these sex-linked conditions from which boys suffer much more often than do girls. *Color blindness* is one. About eight times as many boys as girls are color-blind. Many more boys also have other kinds of eye trouble and various kinds of muscular defects. One of the worst of the sex-linked diseases is hemophilia (the "bleeding" disease mentioned before), which occurs almost entirely in boys. Among conditions of a different nature, stuttering and reading difficulties occur much more often in boys than in girls, but how much sex-linked genes have to do with these conditions is not known.

In addition to being in less danger of having particular sex-linked diseases or defects, girls have

THE UNUSUAL PEOPLE · 103

a big general advantage: If girls and boys should have the same disease or accident, the "chemical factories" in girls' bodies work better to produce the needed prescriptions for cures and recovery. In other words, boys and men have much greater strength in their muscles, and can do harder jobs, but their systems cannot fight off most diseases as well as the systems of girls and women can.

Of course, not all of the extra diseases, defects and physical difficulties of boys which we've talked about can be blamed on their genes. Boys as a rule are apt to be more careless, and to do riskier things, than girls, so that they expose themselves more to diseases and accidents. Nevertheless, there are many ways, as we've seen, in which nature has given better protection to the bodies and health of girls, perhaps so the babies they may have some day will be healthier.

We must always remember, though, that we have been talking about *most* boys and girls, and not *all* boys and girls. There are many girls who are less healthy than boys their age, and who have one or another of the hereditary defects and diseases we have mentioned. But generally speaking, the physical advantages which most boys have— their bigger size, greater strength, and better athletic ability—are balanced by many advantages which nature has given girls. This is well to keep in mind when a girl sometimes feels like saying "Boys always have the best of it!"

We called this chapter "The Unusual People" for a good reason. The conditions we have discussed do not occur too often, and so those who have them are unusual. Fortunately, too, most children today are much luckier with their bodies than many children were years ago. Doctors and parents know much more about preventing accidents and diseases—before as well as after children are born. Young people now grow up in brighter, cleaner, healthier homes; they are given better care and healthier food; and if they do get sick or have accidents, there are many new medicines and treatments which can usually cure them. Even when diseases, defects and abnormalities are due to heredity—as we noted before—they often can be cured or their bad effects lessened.

While there may be fewer children now who are "unusual" in the ways mentioned, there still are many who are blind, deaf, crippled, diseased, or with other defects and handicaps. Whether genes or accidents were responsible, it was just a matter of chance that some children have been afflicted by such conditions and others not.

So if there is nothing importantly wrong with your body or any of its parts or its working, consider yourself lucky. That should be all the more reason why you should sympathize with and try to help those who haven't been so lucky.

## 12

## TWINS

You probably have some twins in your school or in your neighborhood (and perhaps you are one of a twin pair yourself). In any case, you may have wondered about twins, as people always have done. Scientists, too, have been much interested in twins because the studies they have made of them have helped in many ways to understand people in general.

Since only about two out of every hundred children are twins, they may be considered "unusual" —but not in the sense we used "unusual" in the last chapter, that there is anything wrong with them. Where twins have to differ from other children is only in how they happened to be started off in life within their mothers—both together, instead of singly.

There are two main kinds of twins, as you may have noticed. One kind are the "look-alike" twins, who attract the most attention and who always are of the same sex—both boys, or both girls. The other kind are the "look-different" twins. They may be no more alike than any two children in a family, and may be both boys, or both girls, or a boy and a girl. Grouped with twins are the much rarer sets of children born three at a time (triplets), four at a time (quadruplets), and five at a time (quintuplets). In many ways these bigger sets are like twins (which is why they are called "supertwins"). They can be all the "look-alike" kind, or all the "look-different" kind, or they can be a combination of both kinds.

### The "Look-Different" or Fraternal Twins

The twins who are not alike are the easiest to explain. You will remember that a baby is started off when a sperm from the father enters an egg waiting in the mother and fertilizes it. Once in a great while, though, a mother produces *two* eggs at a time instead of the usual one. So, when the sperms from the father race into the mother, there can be *two* winners. One sperm can enter and fertilize one egg, and another sperm another egg. Two babies can then start to grow together.

However, you will also recall that different

# THE TWO KINDS OF TWINS

## The "Look Different" Twins

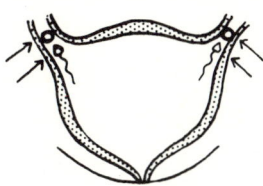

1. These result when a mother produces *two* eggs, and they are entered by two sperms

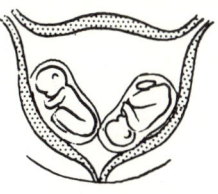

2. The *two different* eggs grow into *two* babies

3. Since they came from *two different eggs*, these twins may be different in all ways, and may be *a girl or a boy* OR *two boys*, or *two girls*

## The "Look Alike" Twins

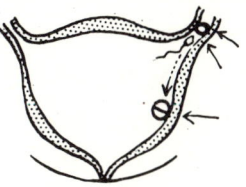

1. These start from *one* egg and *one* sperm. But something makes the egg *split*.

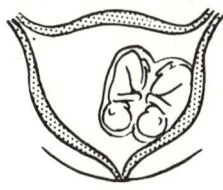

2. Each *half of the egg* grows into a separate baby

3. Since they came from the *same* egg, these twins look alike and are *always two boys* OR *two girls*

sperms and different eggs carry different chromosomes and genes. That is why the babies that develop from the two eggs will not be alike or look alike—any more so than any two children of the same parents who came from different eggs and were born at different times. The two-egg twins can therefore also be a boy and a girl, or two boys, or two girls. Because boy twins of this kind—apart from being born at the same time—are just about like any other two brothers, they are called *fraternal* (the Latin word for brothers). To make it simpler, two-egg girl twins, or a boy-girl twin pair, are also called fraternal.

## *The "Look-Alike" or Identical Twins*

The twins who look so much alike that they can hardly be told apart are the most "twinny." The way they can confuse people, the tricks they can play, and the interesting situations in which they may find themselves, is why they have so often been used as characters in books, plays and movies.

Twins like this are called *identical,* which means "exactly the same." But it is not because they usually look almost identical, or are almost the same in other ways. Sometimes they may look and be quite a bit different. (When we said at the beginning of this book, "There is no one else exactly like you," we meant it to apply even to identical twins.) The reason these twins are called identical is because they came from the *very same fertilized* egg and therefore have *identical*—or exactly the same—*chromosomes and genes*. How could this happen?

Suppose we go back to the time when an egg in the mother has just been fertilized by a sperm, and is about to begin developing into a baby. *Suddenly something causes the egg to split exactly in half.* At the same time, all the chromosomes and genes in the egg also divide into two matching sets, and one set goes into one half of the egg, the other set into the other half. The two halves now break apart, and then take root in the mother's womb, sometimes very close together, sometimes apart. In either case, we now have two babies developing from the same egg.

Since these twins have exactly the same gene workers for everything—features, coloring, bodies, organs—they are almost like one person who has been duplicated and become two persons. That is why they must always be of the same sex—either two boys or two girls—and why they look so much alike, with always the same colored eyes and hair, the same features, and so many other things the same, inside as well as outside of their bodies.

Once in a while, though, identical twins may look and be quite different in a number of ways. How can this happen if they have the same gene workers—exactly the same heredity? That is because (as explained in Chapter 3) heredity doesn't decide everything about what a person will be. Environment—the conditions under which persons grow, and what happens to them—also has much to do with what they look like and turn out to be. And the environments of identical twins are not always exactly the same.

If you are not a twin, you might still imagine how there could be two of you, and different things happened to each "You." So it can be with identical twins. From the very beginning, when they are still inside their mother, one of them might get more food than the other, and become plumper and bigger. Or one of the twins, and not the other, might have an accident in the womb, or something might go wrong inside of him while he was developing. This accounts for the fact that quite often identical twins when they are born are different in size, or look differently, or one is sound and healthy and the other defective or sickly, or not even able to live.

Another difference often found in identical twins is that one may have a birthmark on the right side of the face or body, and the other on the left side. Or one may have on one side a crooked tooth, or the mouth turned up, or an eye a little smaller, and in the other twin it may be on the opposite side. This may be because when the egg from which the twins came was split in half, what was on one side in one half might be on the opposite side in the other half. To understand this better, cut an apple exactly in two, and you will see how the seeds, or the looks of the core, are

## WHY TWINS MAY BE "OPPOSITES"

Cut an apple in half, and you will see how seeds or marks inside the two halves will appear on opposite sides

Since identical twins came from one egg which split in half, they may have birthmarks, crooked teeth, etc., on opposite sides. One may be right-handed, the other left-handed.

reversed in the two halves. Quite often, too, one twin is right-handed and the other left-handed. Sometimes this may be for the same reason that they are opposite-sided in the other traits mentioned, and sometimes it may be for other reasons.

Usually there are enough little differences between identical twins so that members of their family, their close friends and others who know them well, can tell them apart without much trouble. Nevertheless, these twins will be far more alike in many ways than any other two people, and there may be many important things in them which are the same. For instance, whenever a disease or defect is hereditary, and one of an identical-twin pair has it, the other usually will also have it or develop it. This rarely happens with fraternal twins. One reason scientists study twins, therefore, is because they can compare identical twins, who have the same heredity, and fraternal twins, who do not. If something always happens in both twins together when they are identical, but not when they are fraternal, it is good evidence that the condition is hereditary.

But suppose identical twins are different in some important way—in one getting a certain disease and the other not, or one doing certain things differently from the other? Then we know that, since they have the same heredity, the differences must be due to *environmental* causes—to things which have not happened to both twins in the same way. This will help you to understand how in your own case, if there were two of you who had started off with the same heredity, one could still be different from the other.

In other words, the studies of twins show further that what you yourself are is in many ways because of your particular genes—your heredity—but in other ways because of your environment—starting with what happened even before you were born, and then after that, how you were raised, fed, taken care of, treated and educated, and all the experiences you have had. That, of course, is aso true of everyone else.

### *Special Questions About Twins*

*How can you tell exactly whether twins are identical or fraternal* if some identical twins look a little different, and some fraternal twins look a lot alike? There are tests which can be made. Since identical twins always have the same inherited "chemical factories," there are always the same types of chemicals in their blood. If tests show that there are any differences in the blood types, the twins must be fraternal. Further, differences in hair color, eye color, and a number of other hereditary traits that can easily be seen will show that twins are fraternal. Also, fingerprints of identical twins, while never exactly the same, are much more alike than are those of fraternal twins.

*How many children are twins?* In the United States about two in every hundred children are twins. (The average in some countries is a little higher, in other countries a little less.) Thus, in a school with a thousand children there usually are about ten pairs of twins. But some families are more likely to have twins than other families. One reason is that some mothers—particularly as they grow older and have more babies—produce two eggs at a time more often than do other mothers. Another reason is that mothers of different races may carry different genes for twinning, which could explain why there are more twins among Negroes than among whites, and the fewest twins among Chinese, Japanese and American Indians. However, in any race or group of people, "twinning" genes seem to be more common in some families than in others, so one sometimes finds two, three or four pairs of twins in the same family.

*How many twins are identical, how many fraternal?* On the average in the United States, there are about twice as many fraternal twins as identical twins. That is, out of every hundred pairs of twins born, about 65 pairs are fraternal, 35 pairs identical. But as a mother keeps having more children and gets older, there is an extra chance that any twins she has will be fraternal. On the other hand, among Chinese, Japanese and American Indians, a mother is much more likely to produce identical twins than fraternal twins, and so in these groups (who are all of the same race) identical twins outnumber fraternal twins about two to one.

*Do twins have the same thoughts?* People often imagine that because two children grew together in the womb, there must be some kind of special closeness in their minds and feelings. In the case of fraternal twins, this could only be to some extent because, having been raised as babies together, they may have learned to know each other better and so to feel more alike than two singly born children in the family. But in most ways it has been found that fraternal twins usually think and act no more alike than any two brothers or sisters, or a brother and a sister.

It may be different with identical twins. For, in addition to having been born and raised together, their identical genes have produced much the same "thinking machinery." So, as a rule, these twins do think in much the same way about many things. However, they still may differ in their ideas and feelings about other things. Often identical twins prefer different subjects in school, or may pick different friends. (And, of course, they don't later marry the same person!)

*Is there a "mystic bond" between identical twins?* It is another old belief that identical twins have a sort of mysterious "radio" connection, whereby the one can sense what the other is thinking and feeling even if they are far apart. Scientists have found nothing to prove this. The best that can be said is that since identical twins have much the same kinds of minds, and since they may have stayed closely together for a long time, they often surprise people by the guesses they can make about each other's thoughts and actions.

*What are Siamese twins?* These are identical twins who were not separated completely when they started to grow inside of their mother, and so are born with their bodies joined together at some place—the hips, sides or heads. Often these twins can be safely separated by an operation. The name "Siamese" comes from two famous twins of this type who were born in Siam in 1811. Remaining joined together at their sides and hips, they used to appear in circuses many years ago.

*How are triplets, quadruplets and quintuplets produced?* Just as a mother can have two babies at a time, she can less often have three babies at a time (triplets); still less often, four at a time (quadruplets); and rarest of all, five at a time (quintuplets). Any of these sets of "supertwins" can be of several types, coming from one or more eggs. For instance, a set of triplets can come from a single egg which first divided into two parts (as with identical twins), and then one of the parts divided again, making together three babies—all identical. Or triplets can come from two different fertilized eggs, one of which divides to form two babies (who are like identical twins), while the other goes on by itself to produce another baby. Or triplets can come from three different eggs, in which case they would all be "fraternal" in relation to one another.

In the same way it is possible for quadruplets to all come from the same egg which divided and redivided, or from two, three or four different eggs. There are even more ways in which quintuplets could be formed into all identical or all fraternal sets, or into many combinations of fraternals and identicals. However, only a few complete quintuplet sets have survived for long so far, mainly because when there are five babies born at a time, they are so tiny and usually so undeveloped that it is hard to keep them alive. The first all-surviving quintuplets were the famous Dionne girls of Canada, born in 1934. They were a one-egg, all-identical set. Other quintuplets born since then have come from several or all-different eggs.

## 13

## THE WAY YOU THINK

"Now think hard!" someone says to you. You may then knit your forehead, tighten your mouth, squint your eyes and put your hands to your face. That's on the outside. Inside your head you "use your brains."

What is meant by "using your brains"? And how do brains work? We may say that a person's brain works like a combination of many machines. In part it is like the network of tubes, wires and hookups inside of a TV set, bringing in pictures and sounds. In part it is like a tape recorder, taking down everything you want to hear. In part it is like one of those big new electronic computers (mentioned earlier) which quickly put together a lot of facts, figures and questions that are fed into them, and pop out the results and the answers. (You may have seen one of these wonderful machines on TV on election nights. Other such

## 122 · WHY YOU ARE YOU

machines have made possible the flights of the astronauts and the unmanned spaceships and satellites.)

But your brain can do something else. It not only can store up almost everything that is put into it, to use whenever you wish, but it keeps on manufacturing new thoughts and ideas. And the more you exercise your brain, the more it can do for you.

### *Your Memory*

In the principal's office in your school, or in other offices (perhaps your father's, if he has one) you have seen filing cabinets in which are kept

YOUR "MEMORY CABINET"

It's full of everything your brain has taken in and kept

letters, cards with names and facts on them, and other useful information. Your brain too, has a "filing cabinet," which you call your *memory*. In it you file away many facts you have learned, names and photographs of people you know or have met, pictures of places you've been to, and reports of many things that have happened to you. All through your life you will be opening your memory "filing cabinet" to use what you have put away in it (although sometimes things may get lost, or taken out and not put back in place, as in office filing cabinets).

You may be walking along the street, and someone will come up and say, "Don't you remember me?" You'll quickly reach into your memory cabinet and find the answer. "Why, of course! You're Mr. Hoozit, whom I met while my mother and I were visiting the Snaffles three Sundays ago." Or you may find that the person's name has been mislaid in your memory for the moment, and you may look blank until he helps you out.

When you take tests or examinations in school, your memory will give you the answers (or you hope it will!). Your memory tells you not to eat something that isn't good for you, or not to do something which you found is bad for you. Sometimes your memory pops out unexpectedly with an interesting fact that you thought you'd long forgotten.

It is true that some people have better memories than others, perhaps because of better "memory" genes. This need not mean that they are smarter. There are people with unusual memories who are not very bright, and some people who are very bright but do not have good memories. (Sometimes, in fact, depending too much on memory may keep a person from thinking originally.) However, memories have to be trained and exercised, just as do muscles. That is one reason—apart from getting important knowledge—that you are asked to do a good deal of memorizing in school. Even in sports and almost any game you play, you must constantly use your memory. And, of course, your memory will be needed in any job or career you have some day. So *remember*—if developing your memory alone won't make you smart, it will help!

### *Intelligence*

Enabling you to remember, as we said, is only part of the work done by your brain. Your "thinking machine" also constantly takes in new knowledge, and with what has already been stored up, applies it to all the questions and problems you deal with. Everything your brain does and how it works, added together, goes to make your *intelligence*.

Because the human brain is so much more complex than any other organ of the body, and because it also can be *trained* in so many ways, there are very great differences in the intelligence shown by people. The brain of one person may work better and faster than that of another person; or it may be much better than average in certain kinds of thinking. Very often, though, one person may seem smarter than another only because of differences in how they were trained and educated.

For instance, many children in the world cannot read or write only because no one has taught them how. There also are many children who could not answer some questions which you would say are easy as pie. "What is a TV? A telephone? A lawnmower? An elevator? A subway?" Many Eskimo children, far up in certain parts of the Arctic, and many children deep in the heart of Africa, or children in other remote out-of-the-way places, could not answer these questions—not because they aren't smart but because they've never seen any of the things mentioned. But suppose an

## 126 · WHY YOU ARE YOU

Eskimo child asked you, "What is a kayak?" (a kind of canoe), or "How do you make a harpoon for hunting walruses?" And suppose an African child asked, "How can you tell the difference between leopard tracks and lion tracks?" Or "Which jungle berries are poisonous?" If you couldn't give the answers, these children might grunt and say, "What a dunce!"

In your own country, there are children in some other places who may be dumb about many things that are familiar to you, just as you may be dumb about things familiar to them. A farm boy and a city boy may be smart in different ways. The sons of professors, or doctors, or lawyers, or scientists, and the sons of mechanics, or plumbers, or carpenters, or workers at any job, may each know special things which the others do not. Or there may be in your school or class a a child who makes funny mistakes in speaking and spelling English —not because he is stupid, but more than likely because he speaks another language in his home, which he has learned from his parents, and with which he sometimes mixes up English.

There can be other reasons why some children seem dumb when they aren't. A child may have poor eyesight, which keeps him from seeing or reading well. Or a child may have something wrong with his hearing, so he does not understand clearly what others say. Quite a number of known defects and diseases may interfere with a child's work in school. So one often can make the mistake of thinking that because a child is not doing well in his class it is because he hasn't the *brains* to do so.

We must be especially careful how we judge children's *I.Q.s*—the scores made on "intelligence tests," some of which you probably have taken. The purpose of these tests is mainly to find out how well a child deals or will deal with the lessons in school and with ordinary problems. But they may not prove how smart he really is or can be. Some children, or groups of children, may not have had the same advantages in their homes and the same chance as other children to learn many of the things and questions dealt with in the I.Q. tests. If their I.Q.'s are a little lower than those of the other children, therefore, it need not mean that their brains are not as good. With better training and more opportunities for learning, the I.Q.'s of many children could be higher.

### *The Retarded Children*

It is true that some children in all groups and among people everywhere are born with brains that cannot work properly, or in the normal way. Like other organs of the body, brains can also be defective. There may have been something wrong with certain "brain" genes a child inherited, or with one of his chromosomes; or there may have been an accident to his brain while he was developing inside of his mother, or when he was being born. In other cases, diseases may have affected the brains of children while they were babies, or later in the early years. Any of these things could happen to a child of any kind of parents in any group, educated or uneducated, rich or poor, healthy or not.

The children whose brains work poorly or feebly are called *retarded* or *feeble-minded*. They are of many types, due to different causes. Those who are the least below average children are called *morons*. They look no different from other children, and may be intelligent enough to learn a good deal in school, and to work quite well at various jobs. The children with the weakest minds, called *imbeciles* or *idiots*, usually look different from normal children in one way or another, because the same accidents before birth, or the bad genes or abnormal chromosomes, which affected their brains, could also have affected other parts of their bodies. Yet many of these children can learn a good deal, can do useful things, and can be very sweet, gentle and lovable. They may stay at home with their families and go to special schools. But when their minds are too weak they may have to be placed in special institutions.

Finally there are children of another kind whose minds are not weak in any way (they can even be very bright) but who often do not think clearly or behave normally. These are referred to as being *emotionally* or *mentally disturbed*. Possibly in some cases such children may have started off with something wrong with their "brain" genes or "nervous-system" genes. But most of the time the causes were certain things which happened after they were born to greatly upset them and thus disturb their thinking, feeling and behavior. When the causes are found, these children usually can be made fully normal by being given the needed treatment by parents, teachers and psychologists or doctors.

### *Prodigies*

The opposite of children who have very slow or poorly working minds are those who have very fast-working and brilliant minds. You may know an exceptional young person like that (or be one yourself). In the most unusual cases, a child may be extremely far ahead of other children his age in what he knows and what he can do. You may have read of such children, who at the age of nine or ten were already in high school, and at age thirteen or fourteen were going to college. When a child is that far ahead of the average he is called a *prodigy*.

What causes a child to be a prodigy? It may often be not only that his mind works exceptionally well, so that he learns very fast, but also that he has an exceptional memory and so can hold on easily to everything he learns. One girl prodigy I knew had another advantage. She could read in big chunks: instead of seeing a few words at a time, she could see and read a whole sentence. So, as she told me, in two or three looks she could "gobble up" a whole page—and also *remember* it. When she took tests it was like having the school book in front of her.

Sometimes children seem to be prodigies only because they were taught in a special way by their parents from the time they were babies, and read more and study harder than do other children. They may not be able to *think* any better, and so as they grow older they may stop being unusual. But the true prodigies can go on being exceptional all their lives in their work and careers. Many great men in history were prodigies, among them Alexander the Great, Michelangelo and Leonardo da Vinci, Alexander Hamilton, Sir Isaac Newton, Charles Darwin, Benjamin Disraeli, the poets Shelley, Byron and Keats, and many more. On the other hand, most famous men were not known to have been brilliant as children. George Washington was not, nor were most of the other Presidents of the United States, including, most recently, Franklin D. Roosevelt, Harry S Truman, Dwight D. Eisenhower, John F. Kennedy or Richard M. Nixon. And Winston Churchill, one of Great Britain's greatest men, showed no indication at all when he was young of what he was going to be.

So *you* don't have to be a prodigy to be great or famous some day.

## *Musical and Other Talents*

A special kind of prodigy is the musical one—the child who when he is little more than a baby may already show remarkable talent for music. Almost all of the great musical composers, such as Mozart, Beethoven and Handel, were child prodigies. So were most of the great concert pianists, violinists and conductors of the past and present.

In popular music, though, other qualities in addition to musical ability, such as "showmanship," "stage personality," and "knowing what the public wants," play a big part in success. So it is less likely that the talent for popular-music success will show itself in young children. As examples, the Beatles and members of other leading popular-music and singing groups, as well as other recent singing and playing stars of TV and the radio, were not prodigies, and did not attract attention until they were grown up.

A great many people have musical ability. But

## PRODIGIES

Most great musicians were musical prodigies

there are certain ones who clearly stand out above the rest in the way they can compose or play music. These persons, many scientists believe, are born with unusual "musical" genes which can tune up their ears, brains and nerves so they can hear, remember, and play musical instruments in outstanding ways; or who can become great composers or directors of orchestras. On the other hand, in some persons the "musical" genes work so poorly that they can hardly carry a tune. In a few cases these persons inherited defective genes which caused them to be born "tone-deaf": while they can hear other things well, they cannot distinguish between different musical notes. (By now you can be pretty sure whether you yourself have any unusual musical talent.)

There are many other talents and abilities which people may have in different amounts, among them those for drawing and painting, or for writing and poetry, or for acting and dancing, or for science and other professions. But it is harder to be sure about these other talents in young people, since they seldom show themselves as easily or as early as does musical talent. There have been many great artists, writers, actors, dancers, scientists, doctors and leaders in many of the other arts and professions who gave no sign when they were very young of how outstanding they would become in their fields.

You may have noticed that certain talents or abilities seem to run in families. That is, some children may have the same kind of talent as their father, mother or some close relative. It may be possible that a child has received the same "talent" genes. However, if a parent or other member of a family is an artist, or writer, actor, scientist or whatever, a child may have a better chance than other children of being trained for the same art or profession and becoming successful in it. On the other hand, if someone in your family has a special talent, and you do not, this shouldn't surprise you, either. Different members of a family may get different genes. Just as one child may have brown eyes, another blue eyes, the two children may inherit different kinds of talents.

Almost everyone has some kind of talent or special ability: if not for one of the arts or professions, it may be for farming or gardening, machine work, carpentry, cooking, sewing or another kind of useful activity. Being exceptional in this or that sport also requires special abilities.

But having the required talent or ability is not enough. One must also *develop* it, which means having the ambition, the will and the opportunity to do so. Like fine seeds which may not be planted properly, and young plants which are not taken care of, many talents in people never get the chance to blossom and bear fruit.

The first thing to find out, then, is what your best talents and abilities are. Your work in school and the things you are most interested in will offer some good clues. They may not give you the final answer, though, because most young people do not "discover" themselves until they are through high school, or are in college, or even afterward. Often there are surprises. But whatever you eventually find that you can do best and want to do most, one thing is sure: How successful you may be will depend, as with seeds and plants, on how hard you try to cultivate your abilities by study and work.

## 14

## WHAT YOU LIKE AND DON'T LIKE

A young lady I know told me about an odd experience she'd had. She was in a department store buying a new Easter outfit. The junior-miss department was full of girls—and suddenly she noticed that every girl there was buying exactly what she herself had selected: A red coat, red dress, red hat, red stockings, red shoes and a red handbag, each of the same kind and style.

"How strange!" she thought.

When she went outside, she was further surprised to find that every automobile was a red one of the same make and model. And when she reached the street on which she lived, she couldn't believe what she saw—every house had been made to look exactly like her own, painted red and with red drapes and curtains. This astonished her so much she felt herself falling backwards—and *woke up in her bed.*

At once she ran to the window and looked out. The houses were all different, as they always had been. The children and people in the street were wearing clothes of different styles. Best of all, there were two of her girl chums passing by, one dressed in a yellow hat and brown coat and shoes, the other in an all-blue outfit.

"Thank goodness, it was a dream!" the girl said. And you'd agree that the world would be pretty dull if everyone had exactly the same tastes.

What makes your life interesting is that there is such a variety of things from which you can choose, and so many ways in which you can show what you like and do not like. But *why* do you particularly like some things and not others? Did your genes produce a "selecting machine" inside of you, which goes click-click-click when you see this thing or that, and pops out a "Yes" or "No" answer? Or is it all because of what you were trained to like or not like? Or is it a little of both?

### *Your Favorite Foods*

Why do you smack your lips and say "Yummy!" when you see certain foods, and why do other foods make you say "Ugh!"? There may be a good reason if some foods are nutritious and delicious,

# WHAT YOU LIKE · 139

and others are bad for you or don't taste good. But lots of times you say "Yummy!" when someone else would say "Ugh!" Or it could be the other way around. For instance, suppose you were asked to eat a piece of raw walrus fat. You'd very likely say "Ugh! Take it away!" But an Eskimo child would grab it and say "Yummy!"

You may think it peculiar to eat fish raw, as the Japanese do, but you or your parents may enjoy eating raw oysters or raw clams. French children drool over snails, and Mexican children eat fried

A MATTER OF TASTE

caterpillars the way you eat peanuts. There are people who enjoy dining on monkeys, dogs, lizards, grasshoppers, snakes and many other kinds of creatures which you'd be horrified to eat. On the other hand, you might love a juicy steak, but Hindu children would not think of eating it because in their religion a cow is sacred (or thought of as a "mother") and beef is prohibited.

Even among your classmates in school and your own friends you may find that many foods which your family likes would not be served in their homes, or what is popular in their home would not be in yours. Some families like, but others will not eat, bacon, pork, lamb, beef liver, kidneys, calves' brains, shrimp or lobster, eels, catfish and many other kinds of foods. This is because people usually are trained to eat some foods and not others.

In the United States, for instance, many children whose parents or grandparents came from countries in Europe, Asia, Africa, South America or the West Indies have learned to like the particular foreign foods served in their homes. However, a taste for many foreign foods—Italian, Spanish, Mexican, Chinese and so on—has also been developed among Americans whose families have lived in this country for a long time.

Perhaps there are still many kinds of foreign foods which you would not think of eating now. But as you grow older, you may sample these foods in restaurants, or in the homes of new friends, or in countries to which you may travel. Then you may find yourself saying "Yummy!" when you get some of the foods that now make you say "Ugh!"

However, not all of your likes and dislikes about food have to be due to how you were trained. In some cases persons have found that certain foods disagree with them. This may be because of allergies (mentioned in Chapter 10) to any one of a great number of foods, including strawberries, oranges, melons, tomatoes, chocolate, milk, cheese, lobster, shrimp, cereals, garlic, pepper and almost anything you can think of. Various diseases also make it necessary to avoid this or that kind of food. Luckily, most young people are not prevented from eating foods they enjoy—so long as they don't eat too much of anything.

## *Clothes, Amusements, Hobbies*

What has been said about food may help to explain why you prefer (or dislike) certain kinds of clothes, books, music, movies, TV or radio programs, games or sports. In each case it may depend partly on what you have been trained to like, and partly on some of the special tastes you yourself have developed for one reason or another.

Take *clothes*: What you like or don't like to wear now is mostly a matter of style. You may say you want this or that because "all the other kids are wearing it." And you may refuse to wear something else because "all the kids would laugh if I did." But styles change all the time, and what people used to wear may be laughed at now, and what you wear now you yourself may laugh at when you get to be older. So it isn't so much your own feelings about clothes, but what other people think of them, that makes you decide.

Of course, you still have particular tastes which you can show in a number of ways. You may pick colors which you think look best on you. Often they are those which go best with your eyes and hair. But even colors can be a matter of style. People today dress in much brighter colors than their parents or grandparents did. As for the shape and form of clothes—dresses or suits cut one way or another, short or long skirts, hats of this or that kind—it is all decided mostly by what is considered "stylish" in particular times and in particular places. Yet no matter what the style, there is always room for a person's own feelings and charac-

WHAT YOU LIKE · 143

ter to be expressed. So what you wear does tell other people something about the kind of person you are.

What *books* do you like best? Some of them, probably, are among those which have long been enjoyed by young people almost everywhere in the world: *Robinson Crusoe, Treasure Island, Gulliver's Travels, Alice in Wonderland, Pinocchio, Little Women*. But then there are special books which you like most because they deal with particular kinds of adventures, subjects, people, things or places in which you are interested. This is also true of movies, and TV and radio programs. It is these favorites which show how your mind

YOUR HOBBIES

is developing, and which offer clues as to the kind of person you are turning out to be.

Your *hobbies* may also tell something not only about what you are now, but what you may be or do some day. Is your hobby doing experiments with chemistry or electrical sets, or studying things under the microscope? Or collecting rocks, shells, insects, plants or other things in nature? Many great scientists started off when they were young with hobbies just like that. If your hobby is collecting and dressing dolls and sewing clothes for them, or studying the fashion drawings and pictures in magazines, you may some day be a dress designer. If your hobby is working with model airplanes, or operating model railroads, or tinkering with mechanical appliances, you may some day be an engineer or a manufacturer. Painting, drawing, music, writing or photography, are other hobbies which often turn into careers. This is most likely to happen when a person sticks to the same hobby year after year.

Perhaps we have not yet mentioned your favorite hobby. It may be collecting stamps or coins, pictures or other things; or raising rabbits, pigeons or tropical fish; or doing gardening or carpentry; or cooking, baking, sewing or embroidery. Whatever it is, your hobby is not only helping you to have fun, but is surely teaching you much that is worthwhile and practical. Even changing from one hobby to another may be good, in that it gives you a chance to find out what you like best.

Your favorite *sports* and *outdoor games* are different from your hobbies because they require more use of your body. You sometimes find, then, that you prefer the sports or games at which you are better than most other persons your age because you are stronger, or faster, or more skillful. But it is a mistake to look at everything always as a contest, especially when you are young. The main purpose of games and sports now is not only enjoyment or developing your body, but training you to join and get along with others in a fair and sportsmanlike way.

You should also keep in mind that until your body is fully developed, you may not really know how good you can be in athletics or sports. Many stars in baseball, football, basketball and track were not exceptional in sports when they were young, or did not find out until much later that they had the special ability for the sport in which they won great success. But you must not forget that success in sports or athletics, like success in anything else, requires much effort and training, and the desire to succeed.

## Your Friends

If you were the only one who liked certain things, it would be pretty sad. Whether you are playing a game, or watching movies or TV, or having an ice cream soda at a fountain, it's always much more fun when you are with someone else to share your enjoyment. That's what's so nice about having friends.

As you may have found out, the persons who are your best friends now—your real buddies, pals or chums—are the ones with whom you have most in common. That is to say, when you add up all of the most important things you like, your best friends are usually those who feel much the same way as you do about these things. They also may have the *qualities* you believe you admire most or like most in people. In a way, then, the friends you pick tell a good deal about you, too. That is why one often hears it said, "A person is judged by the company he keeps."

You can make mistakes, though, in *not* choosing some boys and girls as your friends. As with tastes in food, your tastes in people may depend a lot on what you're used to. So you may think you don't like certain persons because they're different in some ways from you or the friends you have now. If you get to know those persons better, you may find that the differences are not really so big or important, and may even make them more interesting. Remember, "Variety is the spice of life."

In the years ahead, in high school, college, on vacations or in jobs, you will probably meet and like many new people—just as you'll come to know and like new foods, studies and amusements. Your present friends, too, may change in this way, so you can hold on to many of them while adding new friends to your circle. That will be all to the good. For getting to understand and like more kinds of people is one of the best signs of growing up.

## 15

# YOUR PERSONALITY

The "Seven Little Dwarfs" in the Walt Disney movies and comic books are called Happy, Grumpy, Sneezy, Dopey, Sleepy, Doc, and Bashful. Each one looks different, and has a special way of talking and acting. So each can be said to have a different *personality*.

Personality is, in a way of speaking, the "flavor" of a person. It is everything one notices about a person's character, and how he or she acts with other people. One child may be full of fun, another may be a "sourpuss." One may be a daredevil, another a "fraidycat." One may be bold, another shy. Such traits and many others are all parts of personalities.

How would you describe your own personality? And how do you think you got it? That isn't easy to answer, because everything that has happened to you from the moment you were born has helped to make your personality.

# LOOKS AND PERSONALITY
*All of these notions are wrong!*

 CHINS   BROWS

**RECEDING:**
"Weakness"
"Timidity"

**PROTRUDING:**
"Bravery"
"Determiniation"

**LOW:**
"Low IQ"
"Brutality"

**HIGH:**
"High IQ"
"Loftiness"

 NOSE  NOSE

**UPTILTED:**
"Pertness"
"Impulsiveness"

**ROUND:**
"Geniality"
"Softness"

**SHARP, THIN:**
"Meanness"
"Cruelty"

**LARGE:**
"Virility"
"Aggression"

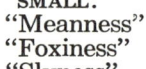 EYES MOUTH

**CLOSE-TOGETHER, SMALL:**
"Meanness"
"Foxiness"
"Slyness"

**WIDE-APART, LARGE:**
"Frankness"
"Honesty"
"Sincerity"

**SMALL, THIN:**
"Coldness"
"Selfishness"

**LARGE, WIDE:**
"Sensuousness"
"Generosity"

EARS  HAIR

**SMALL:**
"Refinement"
"Sensitivity"

**LARGE:**
"Commonness"
"Stupidity"
(if protruding)

**STRAIGHT:**
"Seriousness"
"Placidity"

**CURLY:**
"Frivolity"
"Artistry"

The genes that determine physical traits need not at all be related to the genes that affect personality traits. (See text.)

If there are other children in your family, your parents may tell you that even when you were babies, each of you had a definite personality. Were you the quietest baby or the most restless? Did you smile the most or cry the most? Were you the least bother with eating? Your parents can tell you a number of things about your babyhood personality, and how you may have changed.

## *Mistakes about Personality*

One of the commonest errors people make is to think that this or that kind of eye, hair or skin color, or shape of nose, mouth, ears or body, means that one has such and such a personality trait.

For instance, many people believe that if someone is redheaded, he or she must have a hot temper. This idea may have come from thinking that since red is the color of fire, people with red hair must have "hot" or "flaming" natures. Actually, a redhead is no more likely to be hot-tempered than is a person with black hair or blond hair. And a blond need be no more light-headed or cold in personality than a dark-haired person.

The color of your eyes, or the color of your skin also has nothing to do with what your personality has to be. As was said in Chapter 5, all the colors in human beings are produced by the same kinds of coloring matter, and the differences are due mostly to *how much* goes into the eyes, hair or skin of one person as compared with another. But the amount of this coloring matter has nothing to do with the way people's brains work, or how they are born to behave.

What about your nose? Or ears? Don't they show something about your personality? No. Some people think a snub nose, or turned-up nose, means that one is saucy, or that a sharp, thin nose means that one is sharp and cruel. This isn't true at all. Still another wrong idea is that if a man's jaw is big and his chin sticks out, he must be brave, whereas if his chin is small and pushed back, it means he is timid and easily frightened. There are many other notions about people's faces which are just as wrong. These notions have often come from poems, fairy tales, novels and plays in which writers have used their imaginations. But scientists who have studied the subject have found no such connection as has been imagined between the kind of looks a person may have inherited and this or that kind of personality. In other words, while genes may play a part in producing certain personality traits, any such "personality" genes work separately from the "look" genes.

## *What You Think of Your Looks*

The way in which a person's looks *can* have something to do with his or her personality is in how he or she thinks about them, and how other persons think or feel about them. But the same looks may not always bring out the same feelings.

For instance, when a girl is very fat (though it may be no fault of hers) some unkind children may make fun of her. The fat girl may then become touchy and unhappy. So you may get to thinking that all fat girls have to be that way. But here is an important fact: In various parts of the world—in some countries in Asia and in Africa— it is the very fattest girls whom people admire most. Parents there do everything they can to fatten up their daughters, because they will then be the most popular and get the best husbands. And in those places the fattest girls strut (or waddle) around with their noses in the air, as proud and happy as they can be.

What is thought about a person's height may also depend on where he or she lives. An American boy may feel sensitive when he is a "shorty" compared with his friends. But if he went to some other parts of the world, where boys on the average are much shorter than in the United States, he might be considered tall, and would then feel altogether different about his height. Or a girl may be unhappy if she thinks she is too tall—perhaps taller than many boys she knows—and worried about how it will affect her chances of having dates. But in some western parts of the United States (such as Texas and California), and in Norway and Sweden, and parts of Africa, where there are many very tall girls, her height would not be unusual, so her personality would be different.

Even the way a person thinks of his or her coloring depends on where he or she lives. In some places a girl with light blond hair and blue eyes may be especially popular, because almost all the other girls have dark hair and dark eyes. But in countries like Norway, Sweden and Denmark, the blond, blue-eyed girl would feel she was just "ordinary," since half the other girls would have coloring like hers. Or take skin color. If people act in an unfriendly way to a person because he has this or that kind of skin color different from their own, he may develop one kind of personality. But if people are not concerned with the color or his skin but only with the kind of person he is, he may develop another kind of personality.

A most important fact is that there is no *natural* feeling in human beings for or against any particular kind of coloring, or shape of nose or lips or eyes, or hair form. How children come to feel about particular features or coloring in other people depends on the way they've been trained to think about them.

While it may not be possible to judge personality from features or coloring, a good deal often can be learned from the *expressions* on faces. For example, when people smile a lot and are happy, their mouths and eyes become a little different from those of people who are usually glum and sad. People who are pleasant, friendly and kind to others develop different looks on their faces from those who are mean and nasty. The habit of thinking a lot may show in a face, as compared with the blank look of a person who never thinks much about anything. If you stand in front of a mirror and act out different expressions, you may see how the looks of your own face could become changed if you constantly felt or behaved one way or another.

But always keep in mind that serious mistakes can be made in trying to judge someone's personality by his or her looks alone. The only way of finding out anyone's true personality is by getting to know that person very well and making every effort to understand him or her.

# WHAT MAKES PEOPLE HAVE THESE PERSONALITIES?

## *Certain Personalities — and Why*

Most young people get along pretty well with one another. But there are some who have traits which are considered unpleasant or undesirable. Do you ever stop to think how children get such traits? Let us see what explanations are given by the scientists who study personality, the psychologists.

*The "Fraidycat."* Some children are much more timid about doing things than "nervy" children are. Why? Perhaps a child had an accident, or a severe sickness when he was very young, which made him scary. Or he may not be as strong as other children and not as good at doing stunts, and so may be afraid or ashamed of trying to "follow the leader." Or he may keep imagining what will happen to him if he does this or that. Very often, though, a fraidycat only *thinks* he can't do something because he has never really tried. If his friends don't laugh at him, but encourage him to try, he may be surprised to find that after a while he can do just about everything they can.

We should not forget, either, that *everybody* is afraid of one thing or another. Sometimes the boy who is the bravest when it comes to doing some stunt outdoors, may get all shivery if he's asked to stand up before the class and recite. A famous lion hunter I knew was terribly afraid of sitting in a dentist's chair and getting a tooth drilled. In everyone's personality there may be a little of the fraidycat and a little of the brave. People can often be trained to be one thing or the other. For instance, girls are supposed to be afraid of mice. But many girls when they take biology or psychology in high school or college have to do experiments with live mice, and very soon get in the habit of picking them up and holding them.

*"Show-offs"* and *"Braggarts."* You probably know someone who is always trying to attract other people's attention, and doing it in such a way as to get on your nerves. A show-off or a braggart may act and talk as if he is very important and much better than other people. Actually, he may be really worried inside of himself that people do not think he amounts to much, and so he tries to show that he is a *somebody*. When people make the boy feel that they are interested in him and like him, he may stop being a show-off or braggart. (It's the same with a girl, of course.) However, in some cases a person may really have a special talent or ability—as in playing music, or singing, acting or dance, or in athletics—so when

he calls attention to it, he is not being a show-off.

*The "Bully."* No one likes a big fellow who is always picking on smaller or weaker children. But there may be a reason. As one example, a boy I knew, whom I'll call "Mike," had a younger brother who was much brighter in school than he was, and of whom he was jealous. He was especially mad and unhappy whenever they got their report cards, and his young brother's marks were so much better than his. So he would hit and hurt other younger children because he felt he was getting even. One day, though, Mike's little brother fell through the ice in a pond where he was skating, and might have drowned if Mike hadn't rushed out to dive in and save him. After that the little brother always looked up to Mike as a hero—as did his parents and other people—and a funny thing happened: Mike stopped being a bully, and instead of hurting smaller children, he would do all he could to help them.

*The "Scrappy" Boy.* He is different from the bully because he gets into fights with anybody, even fellows bigger than himself. Why? One of these scrappy boys and his family had just moved into a new neighborhood. The children there were not at all friendly. He thought it must be because they considered themselves better than him, since his parents didn't have as fine a home or as expensive an automobile as the others, and couldn't dress him as well. So the boy may have said to himself, "If those kids are going to be snooty to me, I'll show them who is better!" Before very long, though, he found that he had been wrong. The other children, all of whom had known each other for a long time, were simply taking a while to get used to a stranger; and their parents were waiting to get acquainted with his parents. After not too many months his father was going fishing with some of the men nearby; his mother became active in the Parent-Teacher Association of his school; and he himself became one of the most popular and nicest boys in the neighborhood.

*The "Fibber."* Almost every person tells little "stories" once in a while. But when a child tells big fibs constantly, you may wonder why. Sometimes it's because the child is afraid of being punished if he tells the truth. Sometimes it may be because he doesn't have much fun—or has a lot of imagination—and likes to pretend that exciting things have happened to him. Sometimes he wants people to think he is important. Most persons stop telling lies when they find that it is usually simpler and smarter to tell the truth, and that you get along better with people if you do.

*The "Tattler."* At times it may be necessary to report something bad that a person has done, if it is very harmful or dangerous to others. But some young people are always eager to run to parents or teachers and tattle about the least little act of another child. What explains this bad habit? Perhaps they are having trouble with the persons they tattle about, or are jealous of them, and want to get even. Or they may believe their parents and teachers do not notice or appreciate them enough. So they may wrongly think, "If I tell how bad the other children are, that will show how good *I* am." Many children stop being tattlers when they are helped to become more confident of themselves. They no longer feel, then, that they must get other children punished in order to increase their own importance.

## *How Personalities Change*

There are many other kinds of personality types you may have recognized in your friends and people you know, such as the "hothead," the "smart aleck," the "sissy," the "lazybones," the "stuck-up," the "fussbudget," the "worrier," and others you could name. There also are pleasant personality types, such as "fair-minded," "generous," "kindly," "affectionate," and so on, which may result when boys or girls have been fortunate with their health, family, friends, studies, sports and experiences.

In speaking of personality "types" we have had in mind not a *whole* personality and everything in it, but only some special trait. That is to say, a personality is the combination of various or many traits. In the same person a number of different traits, bad and good, can be found. A person can be a hothead, and yet also generous; or a smart aleck, and yet be kindly and affectionate; a show-off, and yet be fair-minded and sincere.

Heredity may have something to do with personality traits. Some of the hereditary diseases we talked about, such as glandular, nerve or muscle disorders, or some of the allergies, may directly affect personality. Likewise, differences in the "chemical factories" inside of people, caused by genes, may affect their personalities in one way or another. In a general way, some of the personality traits that begin to appear in children when they are quite young may continue in them in later years. Among these traits may be alertness, aggressiveness, restlessness, stubbornness, sociability and the tendency to laugh or cry easily.

However, personality traits do not have to remain fixed. In telling about some of the less desirable personality traits, we tried to show how they develop and can be changed when people get to know and understand one another better. Personality may also change naturally as young people grow older, as their bodies change, and as more education, new experiences and new friendships affect their thoughts and feelings.

You may therefore find your own personality changing a little each year. In fact, even now your personality traits are not exactly the same all the time. When you're sick don't you notice that you are crankier? When you feel blue, aren't you touchier—and don't you then imagine that everyone is picking on you? Aren't you shy with some people and more bold with others? And doesn't it make a big difference when you've felt very lonely, and suddenly you learn there's someone who cares a lot about you?

If there are some things you don't like about your personality, there is a good chance that they will change as you grow older. You may even begin to do the changing now—without waiting—in the ways you'd prefer your personality to be.

# 16

# GETTING ALONG WITH OTHERS

Imagine yourself in a world where nobody cared what anyone else thought, did or felt, and there weren't any rules for anything.

If you played baseball, football, basketball or some other team game, each person would do what he wished, no matter how mixed-up things would become. When you went to the movies, you'd push and shove to get ahead of everybody else. In school you'd never raise your hand but would yell out whenever you wanted to recite. At home you'd never sit down to a table at regular mealtimes—you'd eat when you wished, where you wished, and any old way. You might come to a party with messed-up clothing, a dirty face and uncombed hair. You'd sass grown-ups and talk rudely to everyone. *You'd have no manners*—and neither would anyone else. Maybe that would be fun for a while. But you wouldn't like it for long.

Manners are rules which people work out and observe so they can live comfortably together. The rules you have learned about proper behavior (or *etiquette*) are those which people in your own country or group have decided are best for them. Some of the rules may be different elsewhere. For instance, if you were making a "dress-up" call on a family, you wouldn't think of walking into their house with your shoes off. But in Japan it would be impolite if you did *not* leave your shoes outside, and did *not* walk in with stockinged feet.

You may have been taught it is bad manners for a boy or man to keep his hat on in someone else's home, or in church. But there are a number of religions which require a boy or man to wear his hat (or some other head covering) when in people's homes or in places of worship. For girls and women the rule usually is to keep their heads covered in church (though not in all churches) and sometimes in homes when a formal visit is being made.

While talking of hats, American men might think it peculiar if one man tipped his hat to another man. But in many European countries the men would consider it impolite *not* to tip their hats to one another. In fact, the custom of tipping hats began among ancient knights. When two friendly knights in armor met, each would raise the visor of his helmet (the hinged upper part covering the eyes and nose), so that they could see they were not enemies.

While some of the manners may differ in various parts of the world, the main idea behind them is much the same everywhere: For a person to respect other people's feelings as much as possible, and not to needlessly hurt or offend anyone.

## *Table Manners*

The way you eat—especially when you are with other persons—is a good sign of how "civilized" you are.

It took a long time for human beings to learn not to eat like the lower animals. The very first men, who lived tens or hundreds of thousands of years ago, bit off chunks of meat, or hacked them off with crudely sharpened pieces of stone, and no doubt gobbled the food down with satisfied grunts. Not knowing where their next meal was coming from, when they killed a large animal they stuffed themselves with as much meat as they could eat at once. People then may also have been in the habit of moving off to corners of caves or behind trees and eating separately, for fear someone else would grab their food.

You do not have to worry now about starving the next day, and so you don't have to grab and gobble down what you eat, or sneak off and eat your meal by yourself. What is more, when you sit down to eat with your family or your friends, it is not only to satisfy your hunger. It is a way of bringing you together, to talk over interesting happenings and to help you to feel closer. You often get as much pleasure from the sociability as from the food itself. While people may eat in different ways in different groups—and whether they use this or that kind of knife and fork (or no fork at all, but chopsticks, as Chinese do)—their table manners always have the same purpose, of enabling them to eat together in the most sociable and enjoyable way.

## *Being Fair*

Doing things in a proper and orderly way is one reason for your good manners. Being fair is another reason. When you stand in line for something, or take your turn in following the rules of "first come, first served," that is only being fair. If everyone was always pushing, shoving and fighting to get ahead of everyone else, a good deal of your life would be like a constant cat-and-dog fight.

You also know it isn't fair to fight with and beat someone smaller or weaker than yourself—to be a bully. If no one thought this was wrong, some older, bigger persons might beat up children whenever they wished, and the strong persons might beat up the sick and feeble ones. Even among the most uncivilized people, those who would do this would be punished or treated with contempt. (Of course, our rules permit parents to spank naughty children, but never to really hurt them.)

One of the customs that has to do with fairness is shaking hands when you are introduced to someone, or when you meet a friend you have not seen for a while. (That is, unless you are an Eskimo, for then you might rub noses.) Centuries ago when men always carried weapons, and two strangers approached each other, how could one know whether the other would not suddenly attack him? To show they meant to be fair and peaceful, each man would put aside his weapon and stick out his right hand, then shake that of the other as a sign of peaceful greeting. If men did fight, shaking hands later was the way of showing they were friends again. To this day, when boys or men have quarreled, they may be told, "Now shake hands and make up."

## *What You Wear*

You wear clothing mainly for two reasons: First, to be comfortable according to the weather. Second, to look "right" and "attractive." But do you really wear what you like and what is most becoming to you?

Actually, you may be most concerned with what other people think. That often may mean not wearing what you really would prefer, but what's in style. And to be in style many people may wear what isn't comfortable, or what doesn't look well on them.

Another thing about style is that it can change so quickly, and that what is considered right and attractive can be so different from one year to the next. Some of the clothing boys and girls wear now would have been thought terrible and shocking when their grandparents were young, just as some of the things their grandparents wore at their age might be laughed at now. Even today, how people dress in some parts of the world may look queer or ridiculous to you, just as what you wear or don't wear may look queer or silly to them.

So the only rules for good manners in dressing anywhere and anytime, is that a person should try to look his or her best in the eyes of other people, and not wear what they would consider offensive or improper. This also requires dressing in the proper way for different places and occasions. While your bathing suit might be proper at the seashore, you'd hardly think of wearing it to church, or to a wedding or funeral. When in doubt as to what clothing is correct at given times, your parents can advise you.

Young people sometimes think they are proving their independence by dressing in odd ways, different from the styles of the grown-ups. But if they are *all* dressing in the *same* odd way, what they are really doing is creating and following a new style, so that each one is no longer independent.

One can go too far in trying to be in style and dressing like everyone else. If you know that a certain style isn't right for your face or figure, or is too extreme, or makes you uncomfortable or less attractive-looking, you don't have to follow blindly along. Remember that each person plays a part in setting a style or keeping it going. In clothing as in everything else, you should try as much as possible to *be yourself.*

## The Way You Talk

Sometimes when Americans watch persons from certain other countries, they think it funny the way those people use their hands and gesture with their eyes and mouths so much when they talk. Perhaps you think *you* are different in that way. But notice what you do when you call "Hi, there!" to someone. Don't you raise your arm? And when you say, "Oh, shucks!" or exclaim, "Gosh, that's wonderful!" don't you use your hands and face, and move your body, too? Look at actors in the movies or on TV. You'd be pretty bored with them if only their mouths moved when they talked.

How much or how you use your hands, face and body to act out your speech and feelings depends partly on how and where you have been brought up, and partly on the particular kind of person you are. Sometimes habits of using the hands or face in special ways may be the same in members of a family because children have learned them from their parents or from each other. When there are peculiar, jerky motions of the hands, eyes or mouth which a person can't control, these are called *tics*. Often they are due to nervous conditions, but in some cases tics may be inherited.

(One of the physical oddities—not a tic—which can be inherited is the ability to do tricks with the tongue, as shown in our illustration.)

Your *accent*—how you pronounce words and sounds—is another way in which you may be different from people in other places. People in many countries speak English. But one often can tell by the way they pronounce certain words, such as "this," "that" or "there," or letters such as w, y, s, or v, whether they were raised in the United States, England, Scotland, Ireland, France, Germany, Italy, Russia, or in countries of the West Indies, Africa or Asia. To laugh at someone's

## TONGUE TRICKS

Some people have the inherited ability to curl up their tongues in one of these ways:

  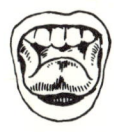 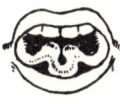

Tongue tip folded up and in Tongue rolled up in mouth Tongue tip turned up and curled on sides Tongue curled up "in cloverleaf" form

foreign accent is foolish. He may be better educated than you, and apart from his accent, may possibly be speaking your language more correctly.

Even Americans from different parts of the United States have different accents, as you probably know. For example, I was born in Kentucky, and started out by talking the way Southern children did. Then my parents took me up North, to Wisconsin, and at first the children there found it hard to understand some of my words. I would say "nawth" when they would say "north." I'd say "po'" when they'd say "poor." And they laughed when I said "hoor-raw" instead of "hurrah." Later I moved to New York City, and found that people born and raised there had accents different not only from those in the Midwest and the South, but from those in other parts of the East. Still later, when I lived in France for a while, and thought I was speaking French very well, I found that most French people knew very easily that I was an American because of my accent.

In your own case, a good "language detective" could probably tell after hearing you talk a few minutes just what part of the country or the world you were from. Wherever you might move from now on, some of your accent will remain with you.

Many people who were fourteen or fifteen when they came to the United States from other countries still have their original foreign accent. How easily one can lose an accent and take on another may depend on one's "ear" for sounds. You may have noticed that opera and concert singers often can sing in several different languages without showing their own native accent in any one of them.

## *Getting Along with Others*

When you are with friends, how often do you say, "*I* want to do that . . ." instead of "Let *us* do that . . ."? A very little child usually talks about "I" or "me," because he isn't likely to think of anybody's wishes except his own. As you become more mature, you will probably think of yourself more often as part of a group, and saying and thinking "we" instead of "I."

The most important difference between adults and children is not that the grown-ups are bigger and more fully developed in their bodies, but that they "think bigger" (or should). A father and mother have to be concerned with many people in addition to themselves. They must think not only of the members of their family and their relatives, but of the people they work with and live with in their communities, and of a great many other people in their country and elsewhere in whom they are interested.

Even if you wanted to be selfish, and would try not to care about anyone else, you could not do so. Other people are part of *you*. Going back a long, long time, what human beings before you have learned, invented and made has been passed on for you to use and enjoy, and to enable you to survive, live and think as you do. So, too, what a great many people in your country and the world over are producing now—not only foods, materials, minerals, chemicals and manufactured things, but also ideas, books, plays and music—is making it possible for you to live, learn and have fun in the way you are doing.

Whether one is talking about one's friends or classmates, or larger groups of different people, or whole countries, all human beings must depend on one another for help of various kinds. No persons, and no groups or countries, can have their own way all of the time. Everyone must often think "we" instead of "I," and must learn to say, "O.K. Let's try to agree on what is fairest and best for all of us." That is the main point in getting along with other people.

## The "Bad Ones"

In every group and place, there always are some persons, young and old, who don't get along in the ways we talked about, and who do not follow the rules of what is fair and right. When their misbehavior goes so far that they make a practice of stealing, robbing and cheating, or cruelly hurting other people, or sometimes committing murder and other crimes of violence, they become known as *criminals*. When those who commit serious offenses are young (perhaps under the age of sixteen), they are called *juvenile delinquents* (de-LIN-quent—not behaving lawfully).

What causes a person to be a delinquent or a criminal? There was a time when it was blamed mostly on "bad heredity." If a father and a son, or several members of a family committed crimes, it was believed that an "evil streak" ran in that family; and if people of some groups had a very high crime rate, it was considered proof that they were "criminal by nature." As we know now, those beliefs are not true. Few if any people are *born* to be bad. In some cases, children and adults who are feeble-minded or mentally sick because of defective heredity may break laws or commit harmful acts. But if they do not realize that what they are doing is wrong, they cannot be called criminals.

However, the big majority of delinquents and criminals are not dull-minded or insane. Most of them have average intelligence, and many are very smart. Why, then, don't they act decently and lawfully? There may be many reasons. Some may have come from miserable and unhappy homes, where they were mistreated; and so they may have begun to think, "If nobody loves or cares about me, why should I care about anybody else?" Or they may have lived in dirty, broken-down houses, and have been so poor they didn't get enough food or proper clothing, and so they may have felt, "If I wasn't given what other children have, why shouldn't I get it any way I can?" And some persons, even if they were not very poor or did not come from bad neighborhoods, may have had unfortunate experiences which make them feel the whole world is against them, and so they are against the world. All of this is bad thinking. Whatever one's grievances, he is not made happier by doing wrong to others.

Among young people, wrongdoing often occurs because some are in too much of a hurry to become like grown-ups, and make the mistake of copying the worst habits of older persons, such as drinking, gambling and being loose in sex behavior. Or they may take drugs for excitement and thrills, to put them in "dream clouds," without realizing that such drugs can do permanent damage to their minds and bodies, and in the case of girls, may be harmful to the babies they may bear some day. Unfortunately, many young people without too much willpower or common sense may imitate the bad habits of others because they think it's in style. But "monkey sees, monkey does" is a dangerous principle to follow.

For the biggest crime in wrongdoing is that which persons commit against themselves. Whether or not they are arrested and punished by the law, they cannot escape their self-punishment. It should not be hard to see that the more one makes a practice of wronging others, the less likely he is to get a proper education, the training for a good job or career, and the chance to work and live happily, form worthwhile friendships, marry the right person and raise a happy family some day.

Yet in any place or group some people are much more easily pushed into criminal paths than others. No matter how bad the conditions, most people go straight; and often in the same family only one member is a bad egg. Possibly, then, there are special weaknesses in the characters of some persons which could be partly caused by genes. If there are any such genes for criminal behavior, little is yet known about them. It has been reported that some men who have abnormal combinations of "sex" chromosomes—two of the "maleness" Ys (plus the X), instead of the normal one Y with an X—tend to be more than ordinarily aggressive, and have a much higher than average chance of committing murders. Most men with this chromosome abnormality, however, do not become criminals.

What *is* known beyond question is that by far the biggest reason for making some persons, or members of some groups, much more likely than others to become delinquents or criminals is *bad environment.* This means, among other things, unwholesome living conditions and surroundings, bad companions, lack of proper care and education, and lack of the opportunity to get good jobs. Thus, without worrying too much about the heredity of this or that person or group, crime can be most quickly reduced by improving the bad conditions under which many people still live, and helping all people to understand each other better and to get along together more peacefully and happily.

# 17

# BOYS AND GIRLS TOGETHER

If you are a boy, you may sometimes have wondered, "What would I be like if I were a girl?" And if you are a girl, you may have thought, "What would I be like if I were a boy?"

These questions really can't be answered, because if there had been a difference in sex, the person would no longer be YOU. Being either a boy, or a girl, is one of the most important things that makes you what you are.

In earlier chapters we have told how the sex chromosomes cause a baby to be either a boy or a girl, and how the bodies of girls and boys differ (with girls in many ways being healthier and having fewer natural defects than boys). Now we'll talk about differences in the way girls and boys behave and think—and the reasons why they do.

## Boys' and Girls' Games

Here is a song you probably know:

*East Side, West Side, all around the town,
Boys and girls together, "London Bridge is
falling down—"*

This song was written many years ago about children in the city of New York. "London Bridge" was one of the games they played (and perhaps you once played it yourself). As the song says, boys and girls played this game *together*. But there were some games played only by boys, and some only by girls, just as is now the case everywhere in the world. It is the same with toys, some kinds of toys being mostly for boys, and other kinds for girls.

You may ask, then, "Isn't there something *inside* the minds and bodies of girls and boys—perhaps produced by their genes—which makes them want to play different games, and to play with different toys? Or is it all because they are *trained* to play differently?" As we will see, it is for both reasons.

To start with, there are some *natural* reasons why boys and girls would not play in exactly the same way. Even among lower animals (as you may have noticed in dogs and cats or other animals you've seen) the little males differ from the little females in how they behave, with the males usually being rougher and more active. So little boys, too, tend to be rougher in their play, more restless, and more interested in things that work (which they soon break up), or that they can push around and make noise with. Little girls, on the other hand, tend to sit still more, and so are more likely to enjoy toys and objects they can hold and play with quietly. Many years ago a woman who trained animals for circuses showed me that this was also true of little male and female chimpanzees which she was raising in her home. (See the illustration.)

In any case, when children are still babies, parents and relatives more often give little boys mechanical toys and things that work or move around, and little girls dolls and toys for quieter play. Pretty soon, too, girls get doll outfits, toy kitchens, and sets of toy dishes or other things their mothers use around the house. Little boys get tool chests, trains, electric motors, building sets, and so on. Some playthings may be the same for boys and girls—skates, sleds, bicycles and games to play indoors. But as children grow older, there are more differences in many of the toys and

## "BOY" AND "GIRL" CHIMPANZEES: THEY BEHAVE DIFFERENTLY, TOO

| YOUNG MALES | YOUNG FEMALES |
|---|---|
|  begin to walk earlier |  better behaved—sit still more |
|  more aggressive |  more sociable<br><br>like to be with people |
|  run away if not guarded |  more deft with hands<br><br>easily learn to thread needle |
|  more destructive<br><br>indifferent to clothes |  clothes conscious<br><br>fond of bright colors |

other presents given to girls and boys. This isn't always because of what the children themselves may prefer.

One of the big reasons for the difference in toys is that both the children and their parents are looking ahead to the future. Most girls are expected to marry some day and have babies and a home of their own. So while it is fun to dress dolls and pretend they are live babies, it also in a way helps to prepare girls for the time when they will be real mothers. Playing at keeping house and helping with cooking, baking, sewing and other such activities is also training for what girls may have to do some day when they marry and have homes of their own.

Boys not only get fun out of playing with mechanical and electrical toys, tool chests, and so on, but at the same time learn through them a good deal that will be useful when they become men. Many boys also help with their father's jobs, and go fishing and hunting, or join in other outdoor activities with their fathers. So in time boys and girls learn to do and like different things.

The fact that boys usually are stronger and better in athletics than girls leads to other differences in the way they are trained to play. Boys like to make their bodies tough; girls do not. So only boys learn to box or to play such rough games as football. Also, in many games that are played with teams, such as baseball and basketball, girls and boys play separately; and in athletic contests boys seldom compete with girls because of the big difference in their abilities. However, one must never forget that many girls are much better at sports, such as swimming, skating, tennis or track events, than many boys.

There is no reason why girls or boys can't or shouldn't take part in many games or sports that are supposed to be only for one or the other. For instance, marble-playing is supposed to be a boy's game, but every year when there are marble-playing contests, quite a few girls win the championships. A boy isn't a sissy, either, if he likes to play some games that are supposed to be mainly for girls. One day I saw some boys making fun of another boy who was jumping rope with girls. The boys who laughed didn't stop to think that prizefighters and professional athletes jump rope regularly when they are training because it is a wonderful exercise for strengthening the leg muscles.

It is interesting to see how girls and boys change in their feeling about playing or being together. When they are very young they don't mind much whom they play with. Before long, though—perhaps at the age of six or seven—boys begin to prefer to play only with boys, and girls with girls. For a few years you may even hear girls saying, "Boys are awful!" And you may hear boys saying that they "can't stand" girls. But soon there comes a time when boys and girls get to be very much interested in one another, and when they join with pleasure in many games and sports, and at parties. In fact, you already know how much more fun it is when there are "mixed" parties.

### *Boys' and Girls' Clothes*

In Chapter 9 we mentioned how boy babies are dressed in blue and girl babies are dressed in pink. The choice of colors, of course, has nothing to do with what the babies themselves want. It is much the same with some of the other differences in how girls and boys are dressed. The kind of clothes you yourself are wearing has depended mostly on the ideas people have now about the way a girl or a boy should be dressed. It may have been different in former days, and it can still be different in other parts of the world.

If you are a boy, you'd probably say, "No one could catch *me* wearing a skirt, or a bow in my hair!" Why not? Only because it isn't the style now. But there were times when boys did wear skirts, just as they often do today in Scotland and Greece. Look at pictures in your history books and you will also see that men and boys once dressed in fancy ways which you now would think were proper only for girls and women.

Brave knights of old, when they weren't in armor, often wore hats adorned with long feathers and ribbons, and silk and velvet coats and robes, and necklaces of gold and jewels. About two hundred years ago, French noblemen wore their hair in long curls, tied with big silk ribbons and sometimes with flowers stuck in them. And some of the men wore lace panties down to their ankles! Even men like George Washington and Alexander Hamilton wore elegant silk and satin clothes, with lace around their collars and cuffs, and had their hair tied with ribbons. Not only that, but when they went to parties they often would paint their faces and make up their eyes. So don't think it's natural for only girls and women to use a lot of makeup, or to fuss so about their clothes.

Come to think of it, ideas of how boys should dress and look have already changed a lot since the days when their fathers or grandfathers were the same age. Some boys are now wearing their hair as long as that of many girls, or dressing in lacy shirts, with chains and beads around their necks, or dolling up in other ways that would have been considered most peculiar not so many years ago. It's mostly style, then, which decides whether and how boys and girls should dress differently. Nevertheless, whatever the style, there will still be differences in the shapes of their bodies, their physical activities, their jobs and their habits, which will always keep the two sexes from dressing in exactly the same way.

### *Which Are Smarter — Boys or Girls?*

If you are a boy, you will probably say, "Boys are smarter." If you are a girl, you may say, "Girls are smarter." Who is right?

No one really knows how the *amount* of intelligence in boys or men compares with that in girls and women. What we know only is that girls and boys do not *think* in exactly the same way. One reason for this, certainly, is that they are trained and train themselves for different kinds of activities, work and ways of living. But there also are differences in their bodies, and in how they grow, which may have effects on how they think and act.

As one example (which you may have noticed

if you have a little sister and a little brother), most little girls usually begin to dress themselves, button their clothes and tie their shoelaces earlier than most little boys at the same age. In general, little boys are clumsier, which may be partly because girls are ahead of them in growth from the time they are born. (This shows up most when girls reach puberty a full year or more before boys do.)

Another difference is that little girls usually begin to talk a little earlier, and talk more clearly and more correctly than little boys. Little girls also are usually better at remembering songs and stories; they learn more quickly to tell the differences between colors; they sit still more and read more; and they pay more attention to what people say, what they wear and how they look. In school, girls continue to talk better and more correctly, to spell better, and to get better marks, all the way through junior high and often until graduation from high school.

But boys are smarter in other ways. They're better in thinking out problems in arithmetic or geometry and working out new ideas of various kinds. They know a lot more about machinery and tools, and how to build and fix things, and they do better in science studies. By the time they're well

# WHO'S BETTER?

Most girls are better at some things than boys are

Most boys are better at other things than girls are

But some girls are better at things boys are supposed to do best

Some boys are better at things girls are supposed to do best

along in high school, more boys are thinking of going into careers and professions, while more girls are looking ahead to being homemakers. So more differences develop in what boys are interested in and what girls are interested in, and how they develop their minds.

When everything is added up, then, it becomes impossible to say that either sex is smarter than the other. What must also be kept in mind is that we are always talking about girls in general and boys in general. In your class at school there probably are some girls who are exceptionally smart at things boys are supposed to know better, such as arithmetic, or science, or how machinery works. And there may be some boys who are much better in language, writing and spelling than many girls, and some who are unusually smart about clothes and colors, or who can even cook and bake better.

There is no reason why a girl or a boy should not try to learn to do the things he or she likes best. No subject taught in school should be considered purely a "boy's subject," or a "girl's subject." For girls, especially, there has been a big change in people's ideas about this. In former times, when few women had jobs or interests outside the home, girls were not supposed to know or learn anything about machinery, science, business, politics or various other subjects which were thought of as strictly connected with "man's world." Many people thought girls and women didn't have the brains for these subjects. But as you well know, women today are in almost every kind of work and profession imaginable. There are women doctors, lawyers, judges, scientists, heads of countries, business leaders, manufacturers, airplane pilots, big-game hunters, explorers—just about everything.

So if a girl is interested in any subject whatsoever, there is no reason why she should not study it. With almost everybody driving cars and using mechanical appliances, and with all kinds of fixing to do around the house, it is very useful for a girl to know about mechanical things, electricity and carpentry, even if she doesn't expect to make a career in these fields. Nor is there any reason why a boy should avoid a subject because he's told, "That's for girls." Take cooking, baking and sewing. Not only do these skills come in very handy at home, but they are needed on camping and exploring trips. What is more, professional cooks and bakers are mostly men, and sewing and designing clothes are jobs which many men do.

## Personalities of Boys and Girls

An old verse says that little boys are made of "snips and snails and puppy-dog tails," but little girls are made of "sugar and spice and everything nice."

Of course, all girls are not one thing in their personalities or characters, and all boys another thing. There are boys of every kind and girls of every kind, and just about any quality you can think of can be found among both. Just the same, there are differences in the ways that personalities of boys and girls develop. We have talked about the differences in their bodies, and how and why they play different games, wear different clothes, and think and learn differently. All of these differences have effects on girls' and boys' personalities.

Girls usually are a little neater and fussier about their clothes, and are more careful about their hair and looks. This may be because they are expected to think more about their appearance. But if girls also take better care of their bodies, it may be for another reason. Some day they may have children, and it is important that a mother should have gotten into the habit of being as neat, clean and careful about her body as possible.

There is also a reason why girls are trained to

be more careful than boys of their behavior, or about people they go with, or where they go. When a girl has a brother of about her own age, she may complain to her parents, "Why do you let Johnny go out alone to the park or movies at night, and not me?" "Why can Johnny stay out later?" "Why can he have a latchkey, and not I?" Parents are not being unfair. It is only because girls are not as strong as boys or as well able to take care of themselves, and run risks that boys do not have of being hurt or misused by strangers or persons who can't be trusted.

Boys are trained more strictly in other ways. For instance, they are expected to act more bravely than girls when there are physical dangers. But boys really may not be any braver. Just as boys and girls may be smart in different ways, they may be brave in different ways. Girls and women may cry more easily, but they are able to face many special dangers with great mental bravery. Also, on countless occasions mothers have risked or lost their lives to save their children in fires or accidents.

You may have noticed that boys are rougher in their talk and behavior than girls; that girls more often show jealousy; that boys more often get into trouble; that girls giggle more; and so on. While these differences may depend a lot on how girls and boys are brought up, there also are natural reasons for some of them. As was said before, among almost all animals the males are rougher in behavior, and also are more likely to get into fights and into trouble.

One other very important fact about male behavior is this: *Males rarely fight with females.* You know that most boys when they near the teen ages could beat up almost any girl who got them mad. But they hold back from doing so. Nor are men likely to beat up women. This is true even among the most uncivilized people. Is it only because boys and men have been trained not to use their greater strength to hurt girls and women, and their fear of being treated with contempt if they did so? No, there is also a *natural* reason for males behaving in a special way toward females.

In just about every species of animal where the male is bigger and stronger than the female, he will rarely fight with her or hurt her, even though he may fight viciously with another male. So one may say there is an instinct for boys when they grow up to treat girls *chivalrously*—meaning like the knights of old treated their ladies, in a gallant, respectful and considerate way.

But the behavior of boys with girls, and girls

with boys, may be most affected by certain other differences which develop in them as they reach puberty. These are the differences in their sex organs, and the acts which involve them. Any young person old enough to read this knows that a girl, after her body has begun to mature, can have a baby if she indulges in sex relations with a boy who is also sexually developed. There are terribly great dangers in this, mainly for the girl—whose body and mind are not ready for such an experience, and will not be until she marries. But there also are dangers for the boy which can affect his whole life. So not only must a girl guard herself, but any decent boy will keep himself from exposing a girl to the dangers. That is a real test of chivalry, even more than not beating up a girl.

There may be many rules for how a girl should act and a boy should act. But when one talks of being a "lady" or a "gentleman," the most important meaning for both is the same: a person who is considerate of the feelings and welfare of others.

## 18
# YOUR FAMILY

Do you ever say to someone when you're peeved, "Oh, leave me *alone!*"? You may mean it for the moment, but of one thing you can be sure—you wouldn't want to be alone for long.

Imagine what would have happened to you if you had been left entirely alone when you were a baby. You wouldn't be here today. Even among many lower animals it is necessary for the young ones to be taken care of for quite a while. But no animals have anything like the long and close relationship that there is between human parents and children.

The nearest to human families are those of chimpanzees and gorillas when they are in their native places in the jungles. The young of these animals may take as much as seven or eight years to become full-grown. That is why ape families stay together much more than do families of dogs, cats, horses, cattle and many other animals, whose young grow up and can go their own ways in less than a year after they are born.

The fact that human children take so much longer than the offspring of lower animals to become full-grown and able to manage their own lives, is only one reason why human families stay together. The most important reason is that human parents *love* their children and are interested in them, in ways that are not true of any lower animal parents and their young. Among cats, for instance, you may have noticed that Papa Tom Cat shows almost no interest in his little ones from the very start; and even the mother, after the kittens are grown, doesn't seem to distinguish between them and other cats. It is the same with dogs and their puppies, or with almost all other lower animals and their little ones.

Luckily, then, human parents want to stay close to their children, and to help them, as long as they can. Children, too, want to be close to their parents. This gives children a chance to learn from their parents some of the most important things in life which are not taught in school. As was brought out in previous chapters, many of your habits, ideas, likes and dislikes, and ways of acting, talking and living, were developed through the training you received from your parents, and from being with them. Most of all, it is through your parents that you first learned how to be loved, and how to love other persons in return.

Perhaps you have wondered sometimes, "How would I be now if I had been brought up by different parents?" That would depend on how different the other parents were from your own. If they lived in the same place, and spoke the same language, and had about the same kind of education and the same amount of money, and felt much the same way about most things as your own parents do, you would not be very different from what you are now. But if the other parents were very different in the ways we have mentioned, you, too, would probably be unlike the person you now are. One way we know this is that when babies are adopted, their language, manners and thoughts become much like those of their foster parents. (In the next chapter we will tell a true story to prove this.)

## *Brothers and Sisters*

Near where I live is a house full of young children. Sometimes you can hear them quarreling and shouting, "I hate you!" or "Go jump in the lake!" or "I could *kill* you!"

Brothers and sisters may quarrel over their toys, or who should do the dishes or run an errand, or what program to watch on TV, or about a hundred other things. The older child may call the younger one a pest or a brat. The younger one may be angry with the older one. A brother may think his sister is awful, and she may think he's terrible. One child may feel that his parents are always picking on him because of another child who's their pet. But if one of the children is ever in trouble, or is abused by someone on the outside, he or she can count on the other children in the family helping and sticking up for him or her. If you have any brothers or sisters, you will find this to be true more and more as you grow older.

What you also will find is that the other children in your family have helped and will help you in many ways to become a better and more successful human being. Through brothers and sisters one first learns how to work and live together with other persons, and not to always have one's way. One learns to understand someone else's thoughts and feelings. A brother who has a sister learns through her a lot about girls, and how to get along with them. A sister who has a brother learns much that is worthwhile about boys, and how to get along with them and make them like her.

An older child in a family can mean a great deal to the younger ones. If a big brother is helpful and sensible, he will be looked up to by his brothers and sisters. And if a big sister is kind and sweet while the younger children are growing, they will always remember her lovingly.

But the older children can also learn and gain a lot from being with younger brothers or sisters. Finding out how smaller children should be cared for will be useful to the older ones when they become parents some day. Also, guiding and working with younger persons is good training for being a leader. A college football coach I know told me, "If I have helped to produce championship teams, one reason is because when I was a boy on a farm I had three brothers much younger than myself. My father was sick and I had to learn how to get my little brothers to work with me, and how to handle them so they did their best and were happy. Today I think of the boys on my team as younger brothers, and they think of me as a big brother. That's why we get such good results together."

While telling how brothers and sisters affect a person's character, one must not forget this: Suppose you are an *only* child? In that case, of course, you will miss some experiences. But you may be able to make up for them in other ways. When a child is the only one, parents usually spend extra time with him or her, and try especially hard to keep their child busy and happy. They usually see to it that he or she always has other children to play with. Sometimes there are cousins who take the place of brothers and sisters. In addition, the only child may try a little harder to make friends, and can become especially smart at learning how to keep himself amused. It is worth noting that only children, as a rule, tend to be above average in school and in their chances for success.

### *Your Other Relatives*

Some of the most enjoyable times in your life may be the occasions when "the whole family" gets together. Ordinarily, family means your immediate family, which consists of your parents, any brothers or sisters you may have, and yourself. Your "whole family" includes, in addition, your relatives such as grandparents, aunts and uncles, and cousins.

Some of your older relatives may be particular favorites of yours. It may not be just because they give you presents, or show they care for you. They also may open the way for you to new places and new experiences. If you have aunts, uncles or grandparents who live in different towns or cities, and you visit them now and then, it is almost as if you had extra homes in different places.

I remember when I was a little boy, living in Milwaukee, Wisconsin, I went with my mother one summer to visit relatives on a farm about thirty miles from the city. It was the first time I'd been on a farm. Everything was so different, new and wonderful. How thrilling it was to see a busy barnyard, all alive with cows and calves, chickens, geese and turkeys; the fields full of corn; the orchards crowded with apple and cherry trees; and the gardens of growing vegetables of many kinds. I even went to a "little red schoolhouse" for several weeks, where there were thirty children in the whole school, all in one room and everybody barefoot—including the good-looking young teacher. That winter my cousins from the country came to visit us in the city, and they were just as excited about seeing the tall buildings, the busy streets, the museums *and* the zoo, where they saw giraffes, hippos, gorillas, monkeys, seals and other animals they'd only read about before.

Even when you visit with relatives who live close to where you do, being with them may in many ways be different from being at home. You may have an uncle whose work is different from your father's, and in which you become interested. An aunt, too, may be doing some work that you like to hear about. And then, perhaps, there are cousins of your own age with whom it is fun to get together. Sometimes, surprises come when you meet second cousins or other relatives you had not known about before.

It is especially exciting if you learn that some famous or important person is related to you. On the other hand, some of your relatives may be poor, unfortunate people who have had troubles of various kinds, and whom your family has been helping. But sometimes it is the other way around. Your parents, or you, or someone else in your family, may need help from relatives. Learning how to help one another in time of trouble, and to do it with kindness, sympathy and generosity, is perhaps the most important benefit that comes to people through their family and relatives.

### *Your Relatives' Heredity and Yours*

"He has his uncle's eyes" . . . "She looks just like her grandmother did at her age" . . . "The cousins could almost pass as brothers."

One often hears how a person resembles this or

that relative. Perhaps someone has told you that you have such and such a relative's eyes, or nose, or forehead, or some other feature. This may have caused you to wonder how much of your heredity is the same as that of a grandparent, an aunt or uncle, or a cousin. Since heredity comes only from the chromosomes one receives at conception, the question then is of how many of your chromosomes are matched by those in the relative you are thinking about. As you'll see, it's mostly a matter of arithmetic.

Let's start with the fact brought out in Chapter 6, that when you were conceived you got half of your father's assortment of chromosomes (one each of his 23 pairs), and half of your mother's assortment of chromosomes. So half of your father's heredity is the same as yours, as is half of your mother's heredity.

Any brother or sister you have also got half of each parent's chromosomes, but not all the same ones you got. From one pair of your father's chromosomes, you might have gotten the chromosome we could call A, while your brother might have gotten the B chromosome. From a second pair, you both might have gotten the same chromosome, and so on. Taking together all the pairs of chromosomes from your two parents, there was a fifty-fifty chance that any of your chromosomes and those of a brother or sister were the same. In other words, you and any brother or sister would have *half* the same heredity, on the average (since it is possible that one brother or sister may have gotten more than half the same chromosomes as you, and another fewer than half).

When we come to the chromosomes of grandparents, aunts and uncles, and cousins which may match yours, we will be dealing with smaller fractions. To make it easier, we'll give the answers, and a brief explanation of how they were worked out.

*Grandparents.* Each of your grandparents has *one-fourth* the same chromosomes (or heredity) that you have. Your father's father, for example, passed on half of his chromosomes to your father, and since you got half of those, half of one-half is one-quarter—the number of that grandparent's chromosomes (on the average) which match yours. Likewise, one-quarter of the chromosomes of your father's mother, and your mother's father or mother, would be the same as yours. However, since you have 46 different chromosomes, and these can't be divided exactly by four, the number of any particular grandparent's chromosomes which you received could have been 11 or 12, on the average, but they may have been a few more or a few less than that.

*Aunts or Uncles.* Speaking only of those who are sisters or brothers of your parents (and not related only by marriage), any one of these is also carrying *one-fourth* of the same chromosomes as yours, on the average. For example, any sister or brother of your father has half the same chromosomes as he, and since you got half of your father's chromosomes, half of one-half is one-fourth. This would apply likewise to any sister or brother of your mother. However, as with a grandparent, the actual number of chromosomes of an aunt or uncle of yours which match your own would average 11 or 12, but could be a few more or a few less.

*Cousins.* A first cousin, who is a child of an aunt or uncle of yours (as described in the preceding paragraph), would have *one-eighth* of the same chromosomes that you carry. Reason: Since the aunt or uncle have one-fourth the same chromosomes as you, and since the cousin received only half of those chromosomes of that parent, one-half of one-fourth is one-eighth. On the average, then, a first cousin might have 5 or 6 of the same chromosomes that you carry.

The facts we've given will explain why certain of your features or other inherited traits may be the same as those of one of the relatives mentioned. It could happen whenever that relative's chromosomes which match yours carried the genes that produce those traits. The closer the relative is to you, of course, the more chance there would be of having genes to produce resemblances. Further, when a gene is *dominant* (or the stronger a gene is in its action), the more chance there will be that you and some of your relatives will have the same trait. That is why certain kinds of eye shapes, or nose, mouth or chin shapes, or certain abnormalities which are caused by extra-strong genes, can show up in many relatives of a family for generations.

## *Your Ancestors*

You may have heard your parents talk about your "family tree," or your "ancestors." As you may know, then, a family tree refers to all of one's relatives going far back, and ancestors usually mean those from whom your grandparents were descended.

Some persons may brag that their family tree is better than anyone else's, so they, too, are better than other people. Or a person may claim he had such and such noble ancestors, and therefore he has their "blue blood" flowing in his veins. How much truth is there in these claims?

First, when people talk about the famous ancestors on their family tree, they are picking out only a few from the great many other ancestors they had. You can figure it out this way: Since you had four grandparents, and each of these had two parents, you had *eight* great-grandparents. Keeping on, the number of ancestors would double with each generation back. (A generation means the

YOUR "FAMILY TREE"

average period—about 30 years—between the lifetimes of parents and their children.) So if an ancestor had lived a few more generations back—say about 200 years ago—there could have been scores of other ancestors living at the same time. Some of them might have been people you would hardly want to tell about.

How much, then, of the *heredity* of any ancestors do you have? To say that one has so-and-so's "blood flowing in my veins" is only a way of talking. Nobody else's blood flows in your veins. Every person makes his own blood. Even when you were being carried by your mother you were making your own blood. Nor is anyone's blood "blue," "noble," "common," or whatever. Every person's blood is red, and blood carries no qualities of mind or character. So when one talks of having some of the blood of certain ancestors, it can only mean that he has (or thinks he has) some of the *chromosomes* of that ancestor—for it is only through the chromosomes and the genes they carry that hereditary traits can be passed along.

Figuring out how many of the chromosomes of a particular ancient ancestor one might have received is again a matter mostly of arithmetic, as when we figured out the matching chromosomes of other relatives. But as one traces further and further back, and the number of one's ancestors grows bigger and bigger, the number of chromosomes one could have gotten from any particular ancestor grows smaller and smaller. In fact, if an ancestor had lived 150 or 160 years ago, you might not have more than 1 or 2 of his chromosomes. If he lived 200 years ago, or before then, the chances are that you don't carry a single one of his chromosomes and may not be tied to him at all by heredity.

Even if you did have a few chromosomes that came from some noted ancestor, it wouldn't mean much, because the genes on that chromosome might have had nothing to do with the qualities for which the ancestor is famous. We must always remember that human beings do not have pedigrees like purebred horses or dogs. No people have been bred for generation after generation, like racehorses or show dogs, to produce certain qualities. On any human family tree, therefore, one can find people of many kinds—bright ones and dumb ones, famous ones and nobodies, good and bad.

This is not to say that having a fine family tree doesn't count for anything. If the ancestors were unusually fine, sensible, hardworking people who did worthwhile things, they would have raised their children in an especially good way, and passed along to them and their descendants some unusually desirable qualities. They also could have had in their heredity many genes which were exceptionally good. So the combination of good training and environment, and some of their good genes, could have been passed along for a number of generations.

On the other hand, it is unfair to think that people who do not have a notable family tree, or do not know about any famous ancestors, aren't worth much. In the case of most people, family records going far back were not kept, or were lost, so they may well have had some notable ancestors without knowing it. Most of the great men in American history—for example, Benjamin Franklin, Abraham Lincoln, Thomas Edison or Martin Luther King, Jr., as well as most of our Presidents —had no known important ancestors. The same can be said of most of the great men of other countries today.

What will decide how important or famous or worthwhile you become is not who your ancestors were or what they did, but what you yourself are and what you do. And some day you will be the ancestor of a lot of other people. Wouldn't you like them to be proud of you?

# 19

# YOUR RACE AND NATIONALITY

You've often heard people speak of *your* "race" or *their* "race" as compared with other races. What are "races"? They are the main groups into which human beings are roughly divided, according to their looks and other physical traits, and the parts of the world where their original ancestors lived.

There are three principal races, one of which is your own: The *Caucasoid* (KAW-ka-soid), or so-called "White" race; the *Negroid*, or so-called "black" race; and the *Mongoloid* (MON-go-loid), or so-called "yellow-brown" race. (Some of the original, nonwhite peoples of Australia and islands near it belong to a fourth race, called the *Australoid*.)

"White," "black" and "yellow" are not good terms to use in describing the different races. As we said in Chapter 7, all human beings have the same kind of brown coloring in different amounts, and no skins are really white, black or yellow. We can better describe the general differences among races as follows:

The *Caucasoid* race is the one to which almost all of the people of Europe and their descendants belong. It also includes most of the people of the United States and Canada and many people of South America, who came from Europe or whose parents or ancestors did. The exceptions are those who are descended from American Indians, or from the black people of Africa. In western Asia, in India, in parts of northern Africa and some parts of South Africa, the people also are mainly of Caucasoid origin.

Caucasoids have been called the "white" race only because *most* of them have skins that are lighter in color than those of other races. But many people of the white race have quite dark skins, and some who live in India or the Arab countries of Asia and Africa, are much darker than many Negroes.

The *Mongoloid* race is made up of the Chinese, Japanese and many other people of eastern and southern Asia, as well as the American Indians (of North, South and Central America), and the Eskimos, all of whom originally came from Asia by way of Alaska thousands of years ago. Most of the Mongoloid peoples have a fold of skin over the inside corner of each eye, which makes their eyes look slanted. They also usually have thick, straight black hair, and very dark eyes. As was said in Chapter 7, this race has been called the "yellow-brown" race because the skins of most people belonging to it are a light yellowish-brown in color, with the skins of American Indians having a little extra reddish, or coppery, tone.

The *Negroid* race is made up mostly of the dark-skinned people now living in Africa, or those living elsewhere whose ancestors came from Africa. Although called "blacks," many Negroes, even in Africa, have brown skins which are not much darker than the skins of some whites, and are even lighter than the skins of certain whites in Asia whom we mentioned before. Most Negroes also have broad noses and thick lips, but many do not.

As you will see, then, one cannot always tell a person's race just by looking at his skin or features. This is especially hard to do when a person is of mixed races. For instance, there are many millions of Americans, and persons in South and Central America and the West Indies, whose ancestors were both white and Negro, or white and Indian, or Negro and Indian, or of all three races together. In Hawaii many of the people are mixtures of the white and Mongoloid races. And in various countries of Europe, Asia and Africa, too, the people may be mixtures of several races. In fact, if we traced back far enough, we would all find that we have some kind of race mixture among our ancestors. There are really no human beings of "pure" race anywhere in the world.

## How Races Began

It may be hard to believe, when you think of such unusual people as African pygmies, that you and they are related in any way. But the fact is that all the people of all the races in the world, no matter how different they may now seem to be, sprang from the same first ancestors, hundreds of thousands of years ago. That is what the Bible says when it tells how all human beings descended from the same first family. It is also what scientists mean when they say that all human beings living today, of all races, are members of the same *species* (SPEE-sheez), which refers to a class of living things who have many special bodily traits in common, and whose males and females can breed and have children (or offspring) together. Our human species has been called *Homo sapiens* (Ho-mo SAY-pe-yens: *homo,* the Latin for "man," and *sapiens*, "intelligent").

The story of how all the differences there now are developed among human beings is a long and complicated one, and we can tell only a little of it here. We will start by saying that just as there are some differences in looks and bodies among members of your own family now, there were differences among members of the first human families, away back at the very beginning. As many years went by and the family groups grew bigger, they began to break up, and some moved off in one direction and some in another. (That is what family groups still do—some of your own rela-

THE HUMAN SPECIES

"MUTATION": HOW A GENE MAY CHANGE

tives having come from, or gone to, a country different from the one where you live.)

When family groups broke up, there may have been some differences in the inherited physical traits of those who went one place, and those who went another place to live. Perhaps it was because the persons of one kind liked certain climates better, or wanted to move off to where they could find more of the food they liked or animals they hunted. In those faraway days people didn't yet have any houses, towns or other permanent homes to tie them down, and no planted fields to keep them in one place. So they could keep going to wherever the hunting was best, the naturally growing fruits and vegetables were most plentiful, and the climate seemed most agreeable. You can see, then, how after a very long time human beings could have become separated into different groups, living far apart on the world's continents and islands. Also, as groups and their descendants multiplied, they became larger and larger; and sometimes two groups came together and formed a still larger group.

Something else had probably been happening. Every once in a while, as scientists have proved, some genes in animals or in people may suddenly be changed or change themselves, (as a result of radiation or chemical or other influences). Such a gene change is called a *mutation* (m'yu-TAY-shun). Genes that had been making skins brown might begin to make them a little lighter, while other "brown" genes might begin to work more strongly to make skins darker. Scientists believe that originally all human beings had skins of about the same brownish color. But in one group of people—those who had moved into Asia Minor (the Near East) and Europe—mutations gradually caused the skins to become lighter. In another group, those who had stayed in or moved deep into Africa, the skins became much darker. In still another group, which had moved farther off into Asia, to the region which is now China, the skins in time became a yellowish light-brown color.

All the while, little by little, some of the genes for eye color, hair color, and the shapes of noses, mouths and eyes also were changing in slightly different ways among the groups of people living far apart. From time to time, too, people of different groups would mix and form new combinations of genes. And so, after many thousands of years, there developed all the different races and mixtures of races that we have today.

Was there any practical reason why the differences in coloring of skin, eyes and hair, or in features, should have developed among the races, or in groups of people living in different places? Yes. It is believed now that certain physical traits may have helped people to live more comfortably, or to survive better, in one region or climate than another. Skin color is an example. Dark skin offers protection against the sun, so that people who had or developed dark skin could live more safely and comfortably in the tropics. (However, even black people can suffer from too much and too long exposure to hot sun.) On the other hand, in colder and cloudier places, very dark skin may block some of the healthful rays of the sun, and so people with lighter skin could live more safely and comfortably in the more northern and cooler regions.

In the same way, dark eyes, with a lot of coloring matter in them, can stand strong sunlight better than light-colored eyes, both in the tropics or in the Arctic, where there is glaring snow and ice. Even thick, black, oilier hair may be an advantage in the tropics or in the Arctic regions.

Certain nose and eye shapes, too, may be better in one climate than another. In the very hot, moist parts of Africa, wider noses help in breathing, while in the cold climates, smaller, narrower noses help to warm up the cold air as one breathes. Perhaps the flatter noses and the "padded" eyelids of the Mongoloid people, such as the Chinese, helped in some ways in the climates where they developed. Other differences in features or in body sizes and forms may have been important to people of different races originally.

But today, when human beings can make themselves comfortable almost anywhere, the physical race differences are no longer so important. There are many ways of keeping warm where it is very cold, and keeping cool where it is very hot. Those with light-colored, sensitive skins can protect themselves against the hot sun with clothing and ointments, and those with light-colored eyes can wear tinted glasses. Dark-skinned people can live and work comfortably and healthfully in the cooler climates. In any race, however, there are certain persons who are more sensitive to weather than others. You may know some who "can't stand the heat," or who "can't stand the cold," and therefore move to other climates. But in general, people of all races can now live almost anywhere in the world, and are doing so.

## *Your Nationality*

While human beings were forming into different races, they also were dividing up in other ways, first into tribes, then, after long, long periods, into nations or countries.

People of various countries—even those of the same race—may have started off with some slight differences in their genes for looks and other traits, because their original mixtures were not exactly the same. In the course of time some further differences may have developed. For instance, the people of each of the countries of Europe—England, Norway and Sweden, Germany, France, Italy, Spain, Russia, and so on—although all of the white race, came to have some differences in appearance, *on the average*. But their differences in language, customs and habits, personality and behavior were due almost entirely to the ways in which they lived and were trained.

You may have heard it said of people of this or that race or nationality, that they are "hot-tempered," or "lazy," or "childlike," or "quarrelsome," or "warlike," or "tricky," or "criminal," or having some other undesirable trait. Sometimes the people of one nation accuse those of another nation of having the trait which they themselves in turn are accused of having. But scientists have found no proof that if any race or nationality has any special traits of character, it is because of its *genes* or heredity. What can produce big differences in the behavior and character of people of different races and countries are their *environments*—the conditions under which they've lived, how they've been trained, and what education they've had or haven't had. When there are changes in the ways that people are brought up and how they live, their behavior also changes.

You can see how this has worked in the United States, where people have come from many countries. At first some of them seem to be very different from native Americans in how they talk and act, the kinds of food they eat, what they read and like to do, and so on. Soon they begin to change, and their children and descendants become like other Americans. You may know how true this is if your own parents or grandparents came from some foreign country. When they first arrived in the United States, many native Americans who

# THE TRUE STORY OF JOHN

**1.** John, a white American baby, is adopted by a kind Chinese man, Ling Woo, in New York

**2.** Ling takes John to his wife in China, where John is raised in the Chinese way

**3.** When John is twenty, a war breaks out in China. Ling sends him back to the U.S.A.

**4.** John says goodbye to his Chinese foster parents and friends, and sails to the U.S.A.

**5.** Arriving in New York, John can't speak English, but talks, walks and acts like a Chinese

**6.** Years later, John looks like a white American, but still talks and acts like a Chinese

saw them may have exclaimed, "My, how strange these people are! How different from us!" But it did not take long for your family to stop being "strange" or "different." And now if you travel to the very country where your ancestors lived, the people there may say, "My, how different that American is from us!"

We have talked about how people changed when they became Americans. But Americans, too, can become different if they are taken as children to live in some other country. One of the best ways of proving this is by the story which follows.

### The True Story of "John" and "Lee"

If you have been to the Chinatowns in New York or San Francisco, or have seen Chinese elsewhere, you may have noticed that many of those who had come from China talk in a different voice, and may walk and act differently from the way you do. You could easily think it is because they were born to be different in these ways. So let me tell you about two young men now living in New York, who are friends of mine. I will call one "John" and the other "Lee."

Lee's parents were Chinese who were born in

California, and who were what one would call "Americanized." Their son Lee was born in New York. He went to school in a white neighborhood, and almost all of his friends were of the white race. That did not change the fact that he still looks like any other Chinese man, with his straight black hair and almond-shaped eyes. But he *acts* and *thinks* like any white American. And if you believe that Chinese are born to have a singsong voice, and to say "vellee solly" instead of "very sorry"—you ought to hear how perfectly Lee talks English.

Now about my other friend:

John's parents were American who lived in a small town near New York City. There was a kindly Chinese man, Ling Woo, who had a restaurant in that town. When John was a baby his mother sometimes came with him to the restaurant, and Ling Woo grew fond of him. One day John's mother told Ling Woo that because her husband had left her, and she was poor and sick, she was afraid she could not take care of her baby any longer. Ling Woo said at once, "I have always wanted a son. Please let me adopt your little boy."

The mother agreed, and so little John—who had blond hair and blue eyes, and looked just like any white American baby—became Ling Woo's son.

Then, to see that the child would be given proper care, Ling Woo took him to faraway China, to a village where he had a wife and two children of his own. John was given a Chinese name, Chan, and was dressed in Chinese clothes. He went to a Chinese school, and lived with the Ling Woo family until he was a young man.

John—who was Chan now—might have remained always in China. But one day the war began between the Japanese and Chinese, and Ling Woo, who had returned to the United States and was now living in New York's Chinatown, became worried about his son. So he arranged for him to leave China quickly.

Now here is an interesting fact. When John, who was by now twenty years old, and who was dressed in American clothes (as Ling Woo had arranged), stepped off the boat in New York, he looked like any average white American young man. But he walked with a shuffle, like many men in China do. He could talk only Chinese. And when he began getting lessons in English, he spoke English words with the same high-pitched singsong voice, and with the "vellee sollee" (instead of "very sorry") accent that you may think is natural with Chinese. Even today, years after his return to the United States, John still does not talk English quite as other Americans do.

It is easy to see from these stories that the way a person acts and talks depends a lot on where he was brought up. If you yourself had been raised from babyhood on in China, and among only Chinese people there, you could have become just like John, talking and acting like a Chinese person. If you had been brought up by French people in France, you would be like any French person. Or if you had been raised in the African jungles by people of some tribe there, without ever seeing anyone from the outside, you would probably be acting like all the Africans around you.

This shows how careful we must be not to jump to the conclusion that if persons of another race or country act differently than we do, it was because they were born to be like that.

### *The Qualities of Races and Nationalities*

It may be good to feel that you and the people of your own race or nationality have certain special, fine qualities. Of course, the people of other races and nations think that they, too, have certain exceptional qualities. But, you may ask, "Aren't those of one race or nationality really *superior* as a whole in their heredity, and born to be more intelligent, more successful and more law-abiding than those of another race or nationality?" Many people like to believe that is the case—especially if they feel sure that it is their own race or nationality which is the superior one. But scientists will tell you there is no proof that this is so.

As noted in previous chapters, we should not confuse what people *are* at a given time with what they *can be*. Throughout history, people of different races and nations have taken turns at being the "superior" ones—the conquerors, the smartest and the most advanced. This happened with the Chinese, Egyptians, Arabs, Persians, Greeks, Romans, some of the Africans, and those of many other racial groups and nationalities.

Two thousand years ago the people living in England and northern Europe (such as the ancient Celts and Picts, and early Germanic tribes) were among the least civilized in the world. When the Romans first invaded Britain (43 A.D.) and "discovered" the inhabitants there (somewhat in the way that Columbus "discovered" the American Indians), they thought them to be hopelessly backward and dull-minded. One of the noted Roman writers, Cicero, advised against buying Britons as slaves because, he said, they were "so utterly stupid and incapable of learning." But how wrong he was! It did take the Britons more than a thousand years to really catch up, but when they did, these supposedly dull-minded people produced Shakespeare and many of the most brilliant writers, thinkers, scientists, artists, statesmen and military leaders the world has known.

In more recent times, mistakes have continued to be made in judging the abilities of people of this or that race or nation. Not much more than a century ago the Japanese were far behind Europeans and Americans in industry, science and everything else that would be considered modern. Many felt sure that the people of the "yellow" races couldn't think and work the way white people could. But in a remarkably short time—once the Japanese turned their minds to it—they became one of the leading nations of the world in manufacturing, industry and the most advanced technical sciences.

In Europe, meanwhile, the Russians, who had been backward in many ways, suddenly roused themselves and in a few decades turned into one of the most educated, technically advanced and powerful of all people. And elsewhere, the Jewish people, who were long thought to have lost the fighting spirit shown by their ancestors in Biblical times, surprised everyone when, in their new state of Israel, their armies proved to have some of the bravest, toughest and ablest fighting men in the modern world.

Some of the worst mistakes have been made in judging the black people of Africa. What may be forgotten is that at the time the British and many other white people of Europe were being started toward advancement by the Romans and Greeks, there were in Africa nations of black people which were much farther ahead in their development. In fact, the black Moors of North Africa were then, and for more than a thousand years after that, among the most civilized people in the world, being leaders in science, mathematics, medicine, art, architecture, philosophy and other fields of knowledge. At a later time, many African Negroes who were forced to become slaves had come from great black nations which had well-developed languages, religions and social systems, complex music and dances, and advanced forms of arts and crafts. Much of the popular or modern music you now hear and enjoy had its beginnings in Africa. So, too, many of the great modern artists and sculptors of Europe and the United States were inspired by the work of black African artists and sculptors.

One may ask, of course, why in various ways the black people of Africa remained behind so many others, and why they are still behind. Among the answers is that at the time modern civilization was catching on and spreading elsewhere, it could not reach to the African people who were cut off by the deserts and jungles. Another answer would be that when the black African people did have contact with those who were more advanced, they were never given an equal chance to become educated and to develop themselves.

Now that opportunities have begun to open up for the black people of Africa, great numbers of them—even some from the most backward tribes—are becoming statesmen, writers, scientists, doctors, artists, professors and scholars. And among the Negroes of the United States, who are descendants of the black Africans, we have already seen the tremendous advances they have made rapidly in many fields as their opportunities for education and careers have increased.

There still are hundreds of millions of people in the world, of every race—in China, India and other parts of Asia, and in South and Central America, as well as in Africa—who are much behind people of the more advanced countries in what they know, do and earn. We can be pretty sure now that their backwardness is not because of something lacking in their heredity, but of what has been lacking in their environments. As the conditions under which they live improve, and their chances to develop themselves become greater, they, too, will become much more advanced.

One of the biggest reasons why human beings of different kinds and groups are kept from helping each other as much as they should, and getting along together as peacefully and happily as they could, is *prejudice*. It means starting off with the fixed idea that every person belonging to this or that other race, nationality or group must have certain undesirable traits which would prevent you from ever being good friends. Only if you are ready to give every person a chance to show what he really is, and to judge him only by what he is, can you be said to be free of prejudice.

There probably will continue to be differences among races, nations and groups of people in their ways of living, thinking, eating, talking, dressing and acting. That may be the results of differences in climates, geography, food and work, as well as in their histories and habits. But the differences should be welcomed. The saying goes, "It takes all kinds of people to make a world." And the world will always be more interesting and exciting if the people are not the same everywhere.

# 20

# YOUR FUTURE

Fortune-telling has always fascinated people. Over the ages it has been believed that one's future could be foretold by looking at the stars... at lines in the palm of the hand... at cards which were dealt out... at a crystal ball... at tea leaves in the bottom of a cup... or by various other means. These forms of fortune-telling may still be taken seriously by some persons, but they can hardly be considered scientific.

Predictions *can* be made about your future without resorting to anything magic, mysterious or supernatural. Knowing something of what you are now—and *why* you are you—one can offer some good guesses as to how you will develop and what you will be in the world which lies ahead. As has been told throughout this book, the person you are is the combined result of what was inside of you—starting with the genes you inherited—and what was outside of you—your environment. And what you can be or will be from now on, and much of what may happen to you, will also depend on what is in you and the conditions, opportunities and events outside of you.

Here, then, are some specific questions you may ask, and answers that can be given on the basis of facts already brought out in this book, plus other facts drawn from many sciences:

*Will your genes stop working once you are fully developed and mature?* No. All of your genes will always continue to be present in each of the billions of cells of your body. They will go on producing their effects throughout your life on your physical functions, your looks, your health, your thinking and your activities. Some of your genes which are governed by "time clocks" will start up or speed up their actions at different coming periods of your life. This has happened or will happen during your period of puberty and adolescence. Later, various inherited traits in your looks, body and mind, and some involving defects or diseases, may appear at successive stages. (For instance, if a boy has inherited a "baldness" gene—which is likely if there is baldness in his father, or his mother's father—it may not begin causing his hair to thin until he is thirty or older.)

*If you have inherited some "bad" genes, can anything be done to change them?* Your genes themselves cannot be changed. (Each gene, remember, has billions of copies in the cells of your body.) But the *effects* of many genes which misbehave can be changed by medical treatments or diets. This has happened with diabetes, and with many other of the inherited diseases, defects and abnormalities discussed in Chapter 11. If you have any inherited disease or defect, the chances are increasing that new medical treatments in the future will provide cures or much reduce the serious effects.

*What will you look like?* Some facts as to how your looks are likely to change were given in Chapter 8. We told how, during or after puberty, there may be changes in hair and eye color, hair form and features, and how family resemblances often increase as children grow older. Are you worried now that you are not as good-looking as you'd like to be? The chances are that you'll be better-looking when you are fully mature. Your mouth will be more shapely, and if your teeth are properly attended to, they will look better. If your skin isn't good (as may be the case during adolescence) it is almost sure to clear up in a few years, and with proper care, you can have a fine complexion. Your whole face may also become more alive and more interesting to others. Your figure, of course, will be more manly or womanly, as the case may be. And one need hardly add that your looks will be much improved as you pay more attention to them, and find out what hairdos and clothing are best for you.

*How will your intelligence change?* Your "mental" genes will soon have done their principal work in constructing your brain. After age sixteen a person's brain is not apt to change very greatly. But how his brain operates, and what he does with it, can change a great deal. As with your body and its muscles, exercise can much improve your thinking equipment and capacities. Also, as you go on with your studies, and as new fields of interest are opened for you, you may find yourself surprised by some of the new things your brain is able to do.

*What can be predicted from your marks in school?* For the time being, your marks may tell a good deal about how well you can handle the usual subjects, how hard you try to do your best, what you are interested in, and how good a student you are likely to be as you continue with your education. But marks in school often do not tell the whole story about a person's intelligence or abilities. For one reason or another, many young people do not try to do nearly as well as they can in school. Later they may become much more interested in learning and getting ahead. Also, a person whose marks haven't been good, or who may not even seem very bright, may yet have what is known as *creativity*—a knack for original thinking or artistic work. Thus, some persons who become fine artists, designers, inventors, craftsmen or good businessmen may not have been outstanding in school. However, the good student is generally apt to be more successful in whatever career he follows later.

*What kind of work will you do?* In former times, many young people did not think much about that question. Sons usually went into jobs, trades or careers not much different from those of their fathers. And all a girl usually hoped for was to marry the right man and become a good wife and a good mother. But today, in modern countries, every young person is free to select and train for any one of a great many jobs or careers. So, you have much more chance to ask, "What would I like to be?" and "What am I best suited for?" Only in rare cases is it possible for a boy or girl to answer these questions clearly and definitely under high school age, or in the first years of high school.

As noted in Chapters 13 and 14, certain talents

and abilities—for music, singing, art, writing, acting—may show themselves at an early age, so that one can predict where a boy or girl is heading. Again, exceptional marks and strong interest in certain subjects, such as sciences, or serious attention to a particular hobby or outside activity, may provide clues to the profession or career a student will follow. But often there will be surprises if you ask your parents, or their friends or other older persons you know, what they originally thought or planned they would be doing as adults.

A girl, especially, may surprise herself and others by what she will eventually do. In former times girls were seldom thought of in connection with careers or professions. But it is different now, and it is likely to be much more so in the future. Many girls may still feel, "What's the use of studying hard in school—I'll get married young and won't have to take a job." That may be a mistake. First, no girl can know when she may have to work for a living, married or not. Further, in the world ahead there will be greater needs and opportunities for women in many fields; there will be fewer distinctions between "men's jobs" and "women's jobs"; and more married women will *want* to do useful and interesting work, or follow careers, outside of the home—at least, after they no longer have to be with their children most of the time. So, if you are a girl, you will be much more likely than your mother was to train for and work at some job or profession. Whatever you do, a good education will also help you to be a better wife, mother and citizen.

*How will your environment change?* The "fortune-tellers" among scientists foresee many changes in the world which will affect your life and the person you are going to be.

—New machines will take over much of the work now being done by human hands. That will make it necessary for you to use your head more—and will require more education and training for mental skills.

—Working hours will be shorter, workdays fewer and vacations from jobs longer. With more free time, it will be more important to have worthwhile outside activities. The more interest you develop in reading, hobbies, music, art, crafts and skills of various kinds, as well as sports, the better prepared you'll be to have a full and happy life in your adult years.

—Because teamwork will become the rule in more and more jobs and professions, it will be highly important for you to understand other people and know how to get along with them.

—Faster planes will carry you more quickly and more comfortably to every part of the world. As your travels increase, it will be of further importance to you to understand and get along with people of other races and nationalities.

—Medical advances will prevent or cure many of today's worst diseases and will help you to have a healthier and longer life. Your "longevity" genes will have something to do with just how long you will live, and good habits will increase your chances of reaching old age. Barring accidents, you and your young friends will probably live much longer, on the average, than any previous generation in the world's history. There should be plenty of time for you to do, see and enjoy everything you wish.

*Will human beings themselves change a lot?* Their genes will not change (or, at the most, very slightly). Human genes have been much the same for thousands of years. Scientists are quite sure that the genes of the caveman and his children were very little different from your own. What has changed enormously has been the *human environment,* as everything people learned through the ages kept adding up to bring them more and more advancement in every possible way. This advancement has been going on most rapidly in our own time, and it may continue at an even greater pace in the future, particularly among peoples who are still backward.

No doubt scientists will find ways to change the workings of various undesirable genes, as we said, and also to speed up the actions of human "mental" genes and improve human heredity in other ways. But there are already in the genes of human beings the capacities and abilities to do far more than they have yet done, and to make themselves much better than they now are. Moreover, the new machines and inventions of the future will certainly provide people with healthier, more comfortable, more exciting lives.

However, the most important changes and advances to be expected or hoped for are those which will enable human beings everywhere and of all groups to get along with one another more peacefully and more happily. That is the main point we have tried to bring out in this book. For by learning as much as you can about why you are *you*, and why other people are what they are, you can help greatly to bring about the improvements which will make the future world a happier one for yourself and for all those who will be living in it with you.

# INDEX

Abnormalities, 93-105
Accents, 173, 174
Adolescence: see "Puberty"
Adopted children, 201
Adrenals, illustr., 88
Africa, Africans, 217, 223, 233, 234
  *see* also: "Negroes"
Albinos, 99; illustr., 94
Allergies, 100, 101, 141
American Indians, 216
Americans, accents, 174
  origins, 225, 227
  traits, 228-230
Amusements, 141
Ancestors, 210-214; "family tree," illustr., 211
  famous, 210-214
Androgens, 90
Anemias, 100
Animals, lower and human, eggs of, 15, 16
  lower and human, 77-87
  disadvantages, illustr., 80
Apes, 79, 81, 199
Asia, peoples of, 234
Aunts, 209

Babies, development before birth, 30-33; illustr., 31
  boy-girl, sizes, 68, 69
Behavior, boy, girl, 194-197

Beards, 75
Beatles, 132
Bible, story of human origins, 218
Birds, instincts, 84
Birthmarks, in twins, 113; illustr., 113
Birth, 32, 33
"Black" race: see "Negroes"
"Black" skins, 54
Blindness, 98
Blood, supposed qualities in, 212
  and ancestry, notions about qualities in, 212
Blood defects, 100
Blood types in twins, 116
Body, puberty changes, 67-76
  workings of, 77-92
Bone defects, 98
Books, preferences, 143
Boy, why you're a, 35-38
Boy-girl differences, before birth, 36-38
  numbers at birth, 38, 39
  puberty changes, 67-76; illustr., 69
  in dress, 67-68
  in bodies, 68-70, 74
  growth, 69-70; illustr., 69
  height, 70-73
  body hair, 75
  breasts, 74, 91

muscles, 74, 75
sex-hormone effects, 90-92
in inherited diseases, defects, 101, 103
games, play, 182-187
behavior, 183, 190
talking, 190
"Who's better?," illustr., 191
personality, 194-197
careers, 241, 242
Brain, 83, 121, 124-131
Braggarts, 158
Breasts, 74
Britons, early, 231
Brothers and sisters, 201-204
Brows, notions about, illustr., 150
Bullies, 159; illustr., 156

Canada, 216
Careers, boy, girl, 193
your future, 241
Cats, parents, 200
Caucasoid ("White") race, 215, 216
"Chemical factory," human, 77-92; illustr., 88
girls' advantage, 103
Chimpanzees, 79, 83
"boy, girl," illustr., 184
*see also:* "Apes"
Chinese, 216, 221, 231
adopted American-Chinese, true story of "John," 227-230; illustr., 226
Chins, 58
notions about, 151; illustr., 150
Chivalry, 196, 197
Chromosomes, human, 23-26
number, 23; illustr., 22
how parents pass on, 43-47; illustr., 44
multiplication of, 45
sex, 35-38; illustr., 37
abnormal, 98; in crime, 180
relatives' and yours, 206-210
ancestors' and yours, 212, 213
Cleft palate, 98
Climate, human adaptation, 82
racial adaptation to, 223
Clothing tastes, 141, 142
sex differences, 187-189
color blindness, 102
Color vision: in animals, humans, 81; illustr., 80
Coloring, human, 49-56; illustr., 52
eye colors, 49-52
hair colors, 51-54
skin colors, 54-56
notions about, 151, 152, 154
mutations, 220-223
Conception, 29
Congenital abnormalities, 97, 98
Criminals, 177-180
Cousins, 209

Deafness, 98
Defects, inherited, 98-103
sex differences, 101-103
Diet, animal and human, 83
allergies, 100, 101, 141
Dimples, 58
Dionne quintuplets, 120
Disease, resistance, 89
inheritance, 98-103
sex differences, 101-103
DNA, substance of genes, 26
Dogs, sizes, 70
color vision, 81
Dominant genes, 48, 53
in features, 58-64

Dress: *see* "Clothing"
Drugs, use of, 179
Dwarfs, 97; illustr., 94

Ear shapes, 60, 64; illustr., 59
  notions about, illustr., 150
Egg, human, 15-18; illustr., 17
  development, 30
  with "X" chromosome, 36-38;
    illustr., 37
  production in girls, 91
  in twinning, 108-110; illustr.,
    109
Elephants, 16, 21
Emotionally disturbed, 129
Environment, 27, 28; illustr., 27
  effects on looks, 57, 63, 64
  effects on stature, 71-73
  crime and, 180
  future changes, 243-245
Epilepsy, 98
Eskimos, 216
Estrogens, 90
Etiquette, 166-168
Europeans, early, 231
Eye, color, 49-51; illustr., 52
  mutations, 221, 222
Eye shapes, 58, 63
  notions about, illustr., 150
Eyes, focus, 81

Face, genes for features, 57-66;
    illustr., 59
  changes in, 64
Fairness, 168, 169
Family resemblances and
    differences, in features,
    looks, 46-48, 58-66; illustr., 46
  in height, 71-73
  in talents, 114
Families, all boy or all girl, 40

relationships, 199-214
"Family tree," 213-214; illustr.,
  211
Father, sperms from, 18, 19, 23;
    illustr., 17
  chromosomes from, 23, 24, 43;
    illustr., 22, 44
  role in sex determination, 35,
    36; illustr., 37
Features, genes for, 57-66;
    illustr., 59
  mutations in races, 221, 223,
    222
Feebleminded, 128, 129
  lawbreakers, 177
Fertilization, of human egg,
    illustr., 17
"Fibber," 160; illustr., 156
Finger abnormalities, 93;
    illustr., 94
Food tastes, 138-141; illustr.,
  139
"Fortune telling," 237
Franklin, Benjamin, 214
Fraternal twins: See "Twins"
Friends, 146
Future, your, 237-245

Genes, human, 22-26
  how they work, 24-27; illustr.,
    22
  varieties, 24-26
  dominant and recessive, 47-48;
    illustr., 47
  for features, looks, 41-66;
    illustr., 59
  unusual effects, 94-105;
    illustr., 94
  for personality, 150-152
  mutations, 220-222; illustr.,
    220

continued working, 238
changes in, 238, 239, 244-245
Genetic code, 26
Getting along with others, 175, 176
Giants, 96; illustr., 94
Girl, why you're a, 35-38
Girl-boy differences: see "Boy-girl differences"
Glands, 88-91; illustr., 88
Gorillas, 79
  see also: "Apes"
Grandparents, 208
Growth, at puberty, 69-73
  boy-girl "growing see-saw," illustr., 69

Hair, body and face
  race differences, 75
  sex differences, 75
Hair color, 51-54; illustr., 52
  mutations, 221
Hair form, 60-62; illustr., 59
  notions about, illustr., 150
Hands, 79
  abnormalities, 93-95; illustr., 94
Harelip, 99
Hawaii, races in, 217
Height, 70-73
  abnormal, 96; illustr., 94
  notions about, 153, 154
Hemophilia, 100, 102
Heredity, definition, 21
  how it works, 23-28
  ancestors and your, 211-213
  relatives and yours, 206-214
Hobbies, 144; illustr., 143 and careers, 242
Hormones, 88-91; illustr., 88
Human beings, future changes, 244-245

Identical twins, see: "Twins"
Idiots, 128, 129
Imbeciles, 128, 129
Indians, American
  skin color, 55
  hair, on body, face, 75
  origins, 216
Instincts, 84
Intelligence, 124-131
  I.Q. differences, 127
  retarded, 127-129
  sex differences, 187-189
  changes in your, 240


Japanese, 216, 232
  See also: "Mongoloid race"
Jewish people, 232
Juvenile delinquents, 177-179


Kidneys, illustr., 88
King, Martin Luther, Jr., 214
Knights, stature, 72


Lashes, 58
Left-handedness, in twins, 114
Likes and dislikes, 137-147
Lincoln, Abraham, 214
Lips, shapes, 62, 63
Liver, illustr., 88
Lobes, ear, 64; illustr., 59
Looks, how you got your, 41-48; illustr., 46
  family resemblances and differences, 41-48, 65
  and personality, 151-155; illustr., 150
  future changes, 239

"Machinery" of body, 77-92

Manners, 165-170
Memory, 122-124
  "memory cabinet," 122, 123;
    illustr., 122
Menstruation, 91
Midgets, 96, 97; illustr., 94
"Mirror-imaging," in twins, 113
"Mirror writing," illustr., 94
Mongoloid ("Yellow-brown")-
    race, 216, 217
  see also: Chinese
Monkeys, 79, 81
Moors, 233
Mother, egg from, 16; illustr., 17
  "seed package" from, 18;
    illustr., 17
  chromosomes from, 23, 24;
    illustr., 31
  baby's growth in, 29-33;
    illustr., 31
Mouth shapes, 58, 62, 63
  notions about, illustr., 150
Muscles, 74, 75
  defects, 98
Musical, talent, 131-133
  prodigies, 131; illustr., 132
Mutations, in genes, 220-222;
    illustr., 220


Nationality, 224-235
  notions about traits, 224-227
Navel, 30
Negroes, coloring, 54, 222, 223
  lips, 63
  hair, body and face, 75
  twins, 116
  origins, 215-217
  African culture, 230, 233, 234
  American, 234
Negroid ("Black") race, 215-
    217

Obesity: see "Overweight"
Only child, 204
Ovaries, 91
Overweight, 75, 76
  notions about, 153


Pancreas, illustr., 88
Parathyroid glands, illustr. 88
Parents, guessing about genes
    from, 47
  human and animal, 199, 200
  see also: "Father," "Mother"
Penis, 38
Personality, 149-164
  looks and, 151, 152; illustr., 150
  types, 156-163; illustr., 156
  changes in, 161-163
  boy, girl, 194-197
Pigment, human coloring,
    49-55; illustr., 52
  see also: "Coloring"
Pituitary gland, 89, 90;
    illustr., 88
Prejudice, racial, 235
Premature babies, 33
Prodigies, 129-131
  musical, 131-133; illustr., 132
Puberty, face changes, 64, 65
  body changes, 67-76
  sex changes, 91
Pygmies, 97, 218


Quadruplets, 119
Quintuplets, 119
Race differences, in color, 54,
    55
  hair, body and face, 75
  in twinning, 116

Races, how began, 218-224
  notions about traits,

qualities, 225-236
prejudice, 235
Reading, 87
Recessive genes, 47-48; 53; illustr., 47
  in features, 60-64
Redheads, 53
"Red" skins, 54, 55
Relatives, 204-210
  heredity, yours and theirs, 206-210
Retarded children, 127-129
Romans, 231
Russians, 232

School marks, predictions from, 240
School subjects, "boy" and "girl," 193, 194
"Scrappy boy," 159; illustr., 156
"Seed package," human, 18; illustr., 17
Sex chromosomes, 35-37; illustr., 37
  abnormal XYY, and crime
Sex determination, 36; illustr., 37
  control of, 39-40
Sex differences, at birth, 38
  in hormones, 90
  bodies, 67-76
  clothing, 187-189
  intelligence, 189-193
  *see also:* Boy-girl differences
Sex genes, 90-91
Sex glands, 90, 91; illustr., 88
Sex hormones, 90
  effects on boy-girl voices, 90
Sex-linked inheritance, 102
Sex relations, 197

"Show-offs," 158; illustr., 156
Siamese twins, 119
Sisters and brothers, 201-204
Skin, color, 54-55; illustr., 52
  mutations, 220-222
  practical value, 222
Skin defects, 99
Species, human, 18; illustr., 219
Speech, 85, 86
  habits, 172, 173
Sperms, human, 17-19; illustr., 17
  sex-determining, "X" and "Y," 35-38; illustr., 37
  production in boys, 91
Sports, 145
Stature: *see* "Height"
Styles, 170, 171
Stomach, illustr., 88
Stuttering, 102
"Supertwins," 119

Table Manners, 167, 168
Talents, 131-135
  and careers, 242
Tallness: *see* "Height"
Tastes, in foods, 138-141; illustr., 139
  clothes, 141-143
  books, 143
  hobbies, 144, 145; illustr., 143
  sports, 145
  friends, 146, 147
Tattler, 161; illustr., 156
Teeth, shapes, 63
Thinking ability, 83, 84
Thymus gland, illustr., 88
Thyroid gland, illustr., 88
Tongue tricks, illustr., 173
Triplets, 119

Twins, boy-girl, 67, 68
  types, 107-120; tests for,
    115, 116
  "look-different" (fraternal),
    108-110; illustr., 109
  "look-alike" (identical),
    110-115; illustr., 109
  "mirror-imaging" in,
    illustr., 113
  numbers, 116
  race differences, 116
  proportion: identical to
    fraternal, 116, 117
  "mystic bond," closeness,
    117, 118
  Siamese, 118
  "supertwins," 119

Umbilical cord, 30
Umbilicus (navel), 30
Uncles, 209
Unusual people, 93-105;
  illustr., 94

Vagina, 38
Voice, mechanism, 85, 86
  sex differences, 86, 90
  types, 86


West Indians, 217
White race, 215; illustr., 219
"White" skins, 54
Womb, 29, 91
Women, careers for, 242
World, future changes in,
  243-245


X chromosome, 36-39; illustr.,
  37
  defects in genes, 102


Y chromosome, in sex determination, 36-38; illustr., 37
  disadvantage, 102
"Yellow" skins, 54